The Not-strictly Vegetarian Cookbook

Written by Lois Dribin

Illustrations and script by Susan Ivankovich

FISHER BOOKS

Publishers: Bill Fisher
Helen Fisher
Howard Fisher

Published by Fisher Books
PO Box 38040
Tucson, Arizona 85740-8040
602/292-9080

ISBN 1-55561-029-3

Library of Congress Cataloging-in-Publication Data

Dribin, Lois, 1947–
    The not-strictly vegetarian cookbook.

    1. Cookery (Natural foods)   2. Vegetarian cookery.
I. Ivankovich, Susan, 1950–   II. Title.
TX741.D75   1989   641.5′637   89-16932
ISBN 1-55561-029-3

Printed in U.S.A.
Printing 10 9

TABLE OF CONTENTS

to the memory of my parents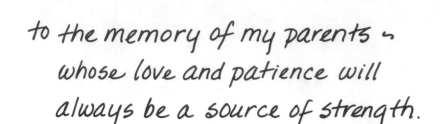
whose love and patience will
always be a source of strength.

Lois

to the memory of my sister, Jeana
her sweet enthusiasm over the
very idea of this book has been
a continuing inspiration.

Susan

INTRODUCTION

This book is really the creation of many people : of our friends in Bucks County, Pennsylvania, who contributed recipes tested at picnics and get-togethers, and chosen as the best of their kind. Of other friends across the country, who sent in recipes famous among family and friends. And of mothers and grandmothers, whose old-country recipes, converted to honey and whole-grain, seem once again "new" and are among the best in the book.

Many of those who contributed have been strict vegetarians at one time or another, or strict adherents of one of the many dietary regimes popular in recent years. While our interest in vegetarianism and healthful eating hasn't disappeared, we have grown more relaxed in our outlook. It seems to us that worrying about food is sometimes as unhealthy as poor eating.

We set out to create a cookbook in which cooking is an enjoyment, not a source of concern. Cooking, after all, is supposed to be a creative affair, not some rigid exercise. The best meals come more often from sudden inspiration than from perfect adherence to a recipe, and we hope you'll use this cookbook in this sort of relaxed spirit.

We conceived of this cookbook several years ago, and worked toward finishing it bit by bit, in between caring for our young (and demanding!) children. We are kind of proud that we finished it, and would like to present it as proof that it is entirely possible to come up with and complete a creative project while at the same time being a full-time parent. Not easy, but possible.

Our basic guideline was simplicity. None of the meals require ten pots or spices only available in Kathmandu! The recipes are such that in a short time, with a minimum of effort, anyone can produce a great meal.

Compiling _The Not-Strictly Vegetarian Cookbook_ has been a wonderful experience for both of us, and has left a real feeling of creative satisfaction. We hope that when you use this book, some of that enjoyment is passed along to you.

Curried Red Lentil Soup

this is an unusual soup — top with a
tablespoon of sour cream or yogurt...
                              truly delicious!

2 cups red lentils
2 quarts water
2 tbsp. butter or margarine
1 onion, chopped
2 stalks celery, chopped
2 cloves garlic, pressed
parsley
1 tsp. curry powder (more, if you like it spicier)
½ tsp. cumin
½ tsp. tumeric
¼ tsp. coriander (optional)
herb salt or salt & pepper to taste
sour cream or yogurt

In a soup pot place lentils — cover with
water and bring to a boil. Reduce heat and
simmer for one hour. In a small pan, sauté
onion, celery, garlic and parsley in butter
for 5 minutes. Add spices and sauté another
5 minutes. Add to lentil broth and cook 1 hour.
Adjust seasoning.

Serve topped with sour cream or yogurt.

Maudie's Chilled Tomato Soup

*... a great way to put those summer
tomatoes to use !*

15 large ripe tomatoes
1 large white Spanish onion
1 small bunch fresh parsley
½ tsp. mild curry powder
salt & pepper to taste
mayonnaise

In a large pot, place about 2 qts. water
and bring to a boil ~ put in whole tomatoes
... when skins split, pour tomatoes into
a colander to cool. When cooled, peel &
chop into small pieces ~ put back into
dry pot. Chop onion and parsley ~ mix
with tomatoes ... add curry, salt & pepper.
Mix well and chill for several hours.

   Serve with a dollop of mayo on top.

Our Onion Soup

3 to 4 large Spanish onions, sliced
½ stick butter
¼ cup tamari (see pg. 237)
3 quarts water
3 tbsp. flour
2 vegetable bouillon cubes
salt & pepper
½ cup sherry (optional)
pinch of basil
½ lb. mozzarella (or jack, Jarlsburg, Gruyere ... ∞)

Homemade Croutons (see pg. 51)

Melt butter in a 4 quart heavy soup pot —
add onions and sauté slowly till dark brown
(do not burn)... they will take a long time to
brown — about 40 min. — but they will brown!
Add flour and mix well. Cover and steam 5
minutes. Add tamari, and water & bouillon
cubes — bring to a boil. Reduce heat and
simmer 1 hour... but the longer, the better!
Season. Add sherry, if desired.

Top each individual serving with a couple
slices of cheese and homemade garlic
croutons.

Split Pea Soup

... my mom once told me that if I didn't
want to use meat in pea soup, I should
try butter ⌣ the winning ingredient, it is!

2 cups dried split peas
2 carrots, chopped small or leave chunky
1 large onion, chopped
2 stalks celery, chopped
2 quarts water
fresh parsley (a handful or 1 tbsp. dried)
a pinch of marjoram (optional)
herb salt and pepper
½ to 1 stick butter
... if you wish, you could add a vegetable
     bouillon cube ⌣ if you think it needs it

In a soup pot, place split peas with water
and start cooking ⌣ for about a half hour.
Then add vegetables and cook 1½ to 2 hrs.
or until split peas dissolve. Add herb salt,
pepper and butter. Serve when butter is
dissolved.

Nutmeg is nice sprinkled on top. I like it
sometimes with & sometimes without.

Hot and Sour Soup

for an authentic Hot & Sour Soup, a chicken soup base is essential. If you have the chicken broth handy, the rest of the soup takes minutes to make.

* 1½ quarts chicken broth (unsalted)
  2 cakes tofu (1 lb.), cut into cubes
  1 large bunch of scallions, chopped
  1 cup chopped Chinese cabbage
  1 large clove garlic, pressed
  12 tiger lily buds (can find in Oriental Market, or check gourmet section of super-market, or gourmet shops.)
  12 dried Chinese black mushrooms (optional) ⟨soak ½ hr. before serving⟩ ...can find where tiger lily buds are sold...
  ½ cup tamari or soya sauce
  ¼ cup sherry (optional)
  2 tbsp. cornstarch
  1 egg, lightly beaten
  1 tbsp. sesame oil (try to find hot sesame oil, but if you cannot locate, use regular sesame and add a little cayenne pepper to soup, to make it hot)

In a large pot, add all the above ingredients except for egg and cornstarch. Cover and simmer 20 minutes. Mix cornstarch with ½ cup water and add to soup. Stir well. Cook another 10 minutes. Beat egg and pour into soup slowly. Mix well and serve.

(con't.)→

~ Garnish with a few chopped scallion greens.

... fried Chinese noodles are a nice addition
to the soup ~ can be bought at supermarket

... a handful of sprouted mung beans are
also good.

This soup is a meal in itself, but you could serve
with Egg rolls (see pg. 128) and /or Teriyaki
Chicken (see pg. 184).

✵ ✵ ✵ ✵ ✵ ✵ ✵ ✵ ✵ ✵ ✵

* When I make <u>Chicken Curry</u> (see pg. 185),
I always have a good deal of chicken
broth left over, which I freeze and
use when needed. If you have to make
broth for this recipe, then save the
Chicken for <u>Chicken, Potato and Broccoli
Salad</u> (see pg. 36) or <u>Curried Chicken
Salad</u> (see pg. 25).

Chicken broth is simple to make ~ just
take washed chicken and put in pot. Cover
with water. Cover. Bring to boil, then
reduce heat and simmer for 1 hour.

Dianne's Manhattan Clam Chowder

- 1 quart clams — shelled (save juice)
- Chop finely and sauté for 5 minutes:
    - hard part of clams
    - 2 cloves garlic
    - 1 large onion
    - 2 tbsp. butter or margarine
- Sprinkle over them and stir until blended:
    - 3 tbsp. flour
- Heat and stir in reserved liquid.
- Peel, prepare and add:
    - 2 cups raw diced potatoes
    - 3 cups cooked or canned tomatoes
    - ½ cup diced green pepper
    - 1 bay leaf
    - ½ tsp. thyme and/or marjoram
- Cover pot ↳ simmer until potatoes are done, but firm.
- Add:
    - soft part of clams

- Simmer 3 minutes more.
- Add:
    - salt & pepper to taste
- Serve with oyster crackers.

... Chowder is always better the second day...

Minestrone

a hearty winter soup — a meal in itself

1 quart canned or fresh peeled tomatoes, crushed
1 cup chick peas
1 cup kidney beans

> soak beans overnight or use cooked beans from the can. I always soak them, as it's more economical and better for you.

2-3 cups water
1 large onion, chopped
3 cloves garlic, pressed
2 stalks celery, chopped (use leafy tops, too!)
½ green pepper, chopped
2 medium zucchini, diced
2 carrots, chopped
1 bunch fresh parsley or 1 tsp. dried
4 tbsp. olive oil or butter (or 2 tbsp. oil & 2 tbsp. butter)
1½ cups uncooked pasta — ziti or elbows
2 vegetable bouillon cubes (optional)
½ to ¾ cup dry red or white wine
herb salt & pepper to taste
1 cup grated sharp Italian cheese — to serve on top

In a large heavy soup pot, sauté all vegetables and herbs in olive oil or butter for 10 min. Add tomatoes. Add water, wine, chick peas, & kidney beans. Cover and bring to boil. Reduce to a simmer & cook 1 to 1½ hours. Stir occasionally. Add bouillon cubes. About ½ hour before serving, add dry pasta and continue to cook till pasta is tender (not mushy) — about 10 min. or so. Add herb salt & pepper to taste. Serve with a generous portion of grated cheese.

Denise's Potato-Leek Soup

a hearty soup — good with some dark bread
and a big salad.

7 large potatoes (leave peels on)
3 to 4 leeks
3 stalks celery
1 large onion
a little basil
herb salt

2 tbsp. unrefined corn oil
1 bay leaf
parsley — a few sprigs or 1 tsp. dried
light cream (optional)
1 to 2 quarts water
(start with 1 quart)

Wash both potatoes and leeks well. Cut major part of the leek's green stem and discard. Chop all the vegetables in large chunks. In a soup pot, pour 2 tbsp. of corn oil and sauté the vegies slightly. Add spices and salt, & at least a quart of water to start. Simmer for an hour or so, till the vegetables are soft. Remove most of vegies with slotted spoon and blend in a blender. Return to the pot and continue to simmer 20 min. Right before serving, add a little cream for richness. You may need to add some more water while cooking, if the soup is too thick.

Cream of Watercress & Potato Soup

10 medium baking potatoes – peeled & cut
1 large bunch of fresh watercress (wash well)
8 scallions, chopped
3 cloves garlic, pressed
3 tbsp. butter
½ cup milk
herb salt or salt & pepper to taste
¼ tsp. tarragon
½ tsp. dill
2 quarts water

Wash, peel and cut potatoes in halves or quarters. Put into a large soup pot – cover with water. Add peeled & pressed garlic cloves. Cover and bring to a boil. Reduce heat and simmer 20 minutes. In a pan, melt butter – add scallions and simmer 5 minutes. Wash watercress well – add to scallions and simmer 5 min. Remove soup pot from stove and with a slotted spoon remove pieces of potato from broth. Blend well in a blender – or use a potato masher and just mash it all right in the pot.) Put pureed potatoes back in pot. Add sautéed scallions & watercress, then tarragon, dill and milk. Cook 5 minutes or till hot. Add herb salt & pepper to taste. Serve. – Garnish with watercress or parsley. You can also add a tbsp. of sour cream to each individual bowl when serving. – This is a good soup if you like to shun dairy.... the potatoes make it creamy!

Vegetable Soup

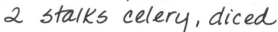

2 cups split peas
1 cup barley
2 quarts water
3 carrots, diced
2 stalks celery, diced
1 onion, diced
3 fresh tomatoes, peeled & chopped ... or
   1 small can tomato sauce
1 large sweet potato, peeled & cubed
1 or 2 parsnips, chopped (optional) –
   (adds excellent flavor)
a handful of fresh parsley
a handful of fresh dill
herb salt & pepper to taste

Place all the above ingredients in a large
soup pot – cover and bring to a boil.
Reduce heat and simmer, simmer,
simmer... for about 2 hours or more.
Adjust seasoning. If soup seems too
thick, add more water.

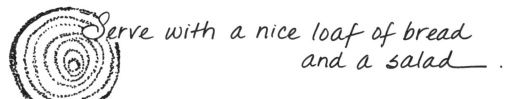

Serve with a nice loaf of bread
     and a salad___.

New England Oyster or Clam Chowder

3 medium potatoes (I prefer to leave the peels on my potatoes ~ just scrub well)
2 carrots, chopped
1 stalk celery, chopped
1 medium onion, chopped
1 clove garlic, pressed

it is not necessary to chop vegies real small, as you will put them in blender when tender

1½ quarts water
5 tbsp. butter
1 pint fresh oysters or clams, with juice
1 cup Half 'n Half
fresh parsley
salt & pepper
herb salt to taste
paprika

In a large heavy soup pot melt butter ~ add garlic and onion, and sauté 5 minutes. Add potatoes, carrots and celery, and sauté 5 more minutes. Add water ~ cover and bring to a boil. Lower heat and cook ½ hour. With slotted spoon remove most of vegies and blend in a blender or food processor. Return to pot ~ add clams or oysters, salt & pepper, parsley and milk. Cook 5 minutes longer and serve.

Sprinkle each serving with a little paprika.

Judy's Cream of Pumpkin Soup

4 cups diced, peeled pumpkin
   (about 1 med. pumpkin or 1 can pumpkin)
3 carrots, sliced
3 stalks celery, sliced
1 onion, chopped
1 bay leaf
6 cups chicken or vegetable broth
1 cup evaporated milk
½ tsp. freshly ground nutmeg
1 tbsp. honey
salt & freshly ground pepper to taste
extra milk

Place pumpkin, carrots, celery and onion in a large kettle. Add the bay leaf and broth. Bring to a boil. Cover and simmer about 1 hour, or until pumpkin is tender. Pass mixture through a strainer, food mill or blender — and return to kettle. Stir in the remaining ingredients, except extra milk. Use the extra milk to adjust the consistency, if needed.

serves 6

Great Gazpacho

↳ what's a cookbook without
a gazpacho recipe... here's ours!

4 large ripe tomatoes
1 green pepper
1 cucumber
1 small red Bermuda onion
1 clove garlic, pressed
1 carrot
fresh parsley
¼ tsp. basil
¼ tsp. oregano
1 cup tomato juice
salt and pepper

Chop vegetables into tiny pieces...
(God Bless the food processor!) Add
spices, salt and pepper, and
tomato juice. Stir well and
chill.

> ...Summer is the time for Gazpacho,
> as it's the time for fresh tomatoes.

Northern White Bean Soup

I cooked this on the wood stove one snowy afternoon
⌐ a good hearty soup

1 cup dry northern white beans (soak overnight or a few hrs. in 3 c. water)
2 qts. water
2 medium onions
3 carrots
2 stalks celery (tops and all)
2 medium cloves garlic
1 parsnip (optional)
½ cup dried soup vegetables (optional) ⌐ ask at your health food store for them ...also sold in supermarkets
1 handful fresh parsley
1 handful fresh dill ← (or 1 tsp. each, if using dried)
2 vegetable bouillon cubes (check health food stores)
herb salt & pepper to taste

Chop all the vegies. Put all the ingredients in a covered soup pot. Bring to a boil. Reduce heat and simmer 3 hours or more. Mash vegies in pot with a potato masher before serving. Adjust seasoning.

Serve with a challah or other homemade bread.

Adzuki Bean Soup

Adzuki Beans are so-o-o good for you...
wonderful for the kidneys.
Buy at a health food store.

2 cups Adzuki Beans (dry)
3 quarts water (1 for soaking)
2 stalks celery
1 large onion
2 cloves garlic
2 carrots
fresh parsley
tamari to taste
2 tbsp. oil
a little seaweed (optional)

Cover beans with 1 quart of water and let soak overnight. In morning, remove water (discarding this water helps eliminate gas). Put in 2 qts. of fresh water and cook in a covered pot for 1 hour. Then sauté vegetables in oil for 5 minutes. Add to beans and cook 1 hour longer. Add tamari to taste.

Serve with a crusty whole wheat bread or with brown rice. See how good it makes you feel!

Tomato Soup

I made this soup with fresh Italian plum tomatoes from my garden.... which I believe is the reason why it was so good.

- 2 lbs. fresh peeled tomatoes (or canned)
- 1 medium onion, chopped
- 1 large clove garlic, pressed
- 1 carrot, sliced
- 1 stalk celery, diced
- 1 small bunch fresh parsley or 1 tsp. dried
- 1 leaf fresh basil or ½ tsp. dried
- 1 head fresh dill or 1 tsp. dried
- 1 or 2 leaves coriander or ¼ tsp. dried (optional)
- 2 tbsp. butter
- ½ cup sherry
- 1 quart water
- herb salt & pepper to taste
- 2 vegetable bouillon cubes (optional)
- 1 cup Half 'n Half

NOTE: To remove skins from tomatoes, place in boiling hot water till skins wrinkle and pop ~ about 5 min. Cool & peel skins.

Mash tomatoes with a potato masher or hands into a soup pot. Begin to simmer. In a small pan, sauté in butter... onion, garlic, celery, carrots & parsley. Add herbs. Sauté about 5 to 10 minutes ~ then add to tomatoes. Stir in water and sherry, and cook 1 hour. Add salt and pepper and bouillon cubes. Simmer 15 minutes. Add Half 'n Half right before serving.

Serve plain or with homemade croutons (see pg. 51).

...this is not a thick soup, so you can cut down on the water if you like it thicker.

Spring Bisque Soup

this is a great soup ~ it's pureed, so the kids can't see the hunks of vegetables! Basically, it's a creamed vegetable soup, so you can use any ones that you like. I prefer.....

1 bunch fresh asparagus
2 carrots
1 medium zucchini
2 stalks celery
5 small potatoes
1 onion
1 large clove garlic
1 bunch parsley
1 cup Half 'n Half or milk

½ to 1 stick butter
¼ to ½ lb. cheddar cheese
½ cup sherry
2 quarts water
2 vegetable bouillon cubes (optional)
herb salt
pinch of summer savory
pinch of marjoram ← (optional)
paprika

In a large soup pot, melt butter and add all your vegetables (leave in large pieces as you will fish them out later to puree). Sauté vegetables 10 minutes. Add water and bring to a boil. Reduce heat and simmer ½ hour. With slotted spoon, remove vegies and puree in a blender or food processor till smooth. Return to pot and simmer another ½ hour. Add sherry, cheese, Half 'n Half, bouillon and seasonings ~ and simmer another 10 minutes. Do not let boil again, if possible. Garnish with a sprinkle of paprika.

~ Serve with a hearty bread.

serves 4

Eden's Lima Bean Soup
~ a different and great soup !

1 cup baby lima beans (soak overnight in 3 c. water)
1 large onion, sliced
3 stalks celery, sliced
1 bay leaf
½ cup tahini (see pg. 237)
1 tbsp. roasted sesame seeds
2 tbsp. parsley
herb salt to taste
¼ cup tamari
dash of basil and chives
1 quart water

Place soaked beans with the water in soup pot. (Use at least 1 qt. water to start.) Bring to boil, then lower to a simmer for 1½ hrs. or so. Then add the rest of ingredients, except tahini. Cook for another hour or till all the beans have softened into the stock. Add tahini 15 minutes before serving. Stir well. Lima bean soup is best cooked slowly for 3 hours or so. You may have to add more water as it cooks ~ if it looks too thick.

Salads and Salad Dressings

Unique Cucumber & Onion Salad

... with feta & sour cream

4 medium cucumbers, ⌐ peel & slice in rounds
    (leave skins on if organically grown)
1 lg. sweet Spanish onion ⌐ cut in thin rings
¼ lb. feta cheese
1 cup sour cream
½ cup vinegar (apple cider or others)
salt & pepper

Slice cukes and onion, and place in a bowl.
Pour vinegar on top. Mix well. Add salt &
pepper. Refrigerate 1 hour, turning a few
times to marinate. Drain off vinegar.
Mix cukes and onions with sour cream.
Crumble feta cheese on top and serve.

You can use Bleu Cheese in place
    of feta, if you like.

Myra's Tofu Salad

2 or 3 cakes of tofu (1 lb.), cut into small cubes
1 large clove garlic, pressed
1 small red Bermuda onion, diced
1 stalk celery, diced
1 carrot, grated or diced
3 heaping tbsp. mayonnaise (give or take a little)
fresh parsley
herb salt
tamari
2 tbsp. oil

In a skillet, heat oil – put in garlic and tofu, and sauté until nice and crispy. Remove and put in a bowl. Chop vegetables and add to tofu with mayo and herb salt, along with a touch of tamari. Stir well and refrigerate several hours.

Serve in the summer with a green salad and buttered corn-on-the-cob!

serves 4

Apple Walnut Salad

... this is a simple, light dessert to put together when you *need* a dessert but don't have time for anything elaborate.

4   apples
½   cup walnuts
½   cup raisins
1   cup apple yogurt

Wash and slice apples — into bite-size pieces. Add walnuts, raisins and yogurt. Mix well. Chill and serve.

⌣ also makes a good breakfast
                or lunch !

Curried Chicken Salad

serve on a bed of lettuce with sliced tomatoes and cucumbers on a hot summer's day.

1 cooked and diced chicken (save and freeze broth for other dishes)
1 cup chopped celery
½ cup chopped scallions (optional)
1 cup chopped seedless green grapes or
       1 cup raisins

½ cup mayonnaise
½ cup sour cream
1 tbsp. lemon juice
2 tsp. curry powder
½ tsp. cumin
½ tsp. tumeric   } optional
salt to taste
parsley for garnish

In a covered soup pot, cover chicken with water and bring to a boil ⁓ reduce heat and simmer 1 hour. Remove chicken from pot ⁓ place in a bowl and let cool (and don't forget to save that broth … freeze it or refrigerate when cooled). Remove chicken from bone ⁓ dice and place in a large bowl … add celery, scallions & grapes (if using raisins, soak 5 min. in water to plump up … drain and add to chicken). In a small bowl mix mayo, sour cream, lemon juice, curry & other spices. Mix well. Pour over chicken salad ⁓ toss well. Refrigerate several hours. Garnish with parsley.

Indian Cucumber Raita
❀ Yogurt Salad ❀

2 cucumbers, sliced
1 cup plain yogurt
½ tsp. cumin
herb salt, if desired

Combine ingredients in a bowl and chill. Serve with curry dishes, as it cools the palate when the curry is hot.

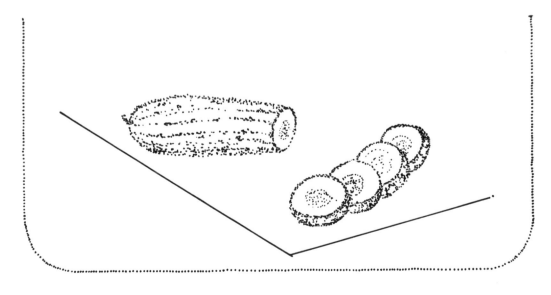

Chilled Poached Haddock Salad

this is a wonderful summer dinner —
served with a green salad & corn-on-the-cob

Poached Fish:

    2 lbs. haddock (I allow ½ lb. per person when serving fish)
    1 small onion
    1 stalk celery
    1 lemon
    salt & pepper

Sauce:

    ¾ cup mayonnaise
    ¼ cup chili sauce (or Ketchup)
    1 hard boiled egg, mashed

To poach fish, place 1 onion & 1 stalk celery into a skillet and fill ⅔ with water — bring to boil. Place fish in water and simmer 5 to 10 minutes (till it flakes with a fork; do not overcook, as it will get too chewy). Drain off water; discard onion and celery and place fish in a bowl to cool. Squeeze lemon over it and sprinkle with salt & pepper... (you don't have to use salt, but pepper gives it a great flavor). With fingers, flake the fish into small pieces, searching for bones while doing so. Discard bones. Chill for at least 2 hours.

Dressing — put mayonnaise, chili sauce & mashed egg in bowl...and mix. Serve with fish.

Summer Cottage Cheese Salad

... very refreshing ↳ serve with a nice cold fruit salad when it's too hot for anything else.

1 lb. creamed cottage cheese
1 large grated carrot
¾ cup raisins

Mix together and serve. Sprinkle toasted wheat germ on top (optional).

↳ Simple and Light ↰ !

Wendy's Rice Salad

~ what a refreshing way to serve rice!

2 cups cooked and chilled brown rice
1 cup chopped carrots
½ cup shredded red cabbage
2 large cloves garlic, pressed
juice of 1 lemon
⅛ cup tamari or soya sauce
½ cup fresh chopped parsley

Cook rice and chill well. Add remaining ingredients and mix well.

You can also add:

onions
cherry tomatoes
avocado slices
celery
green peppers
mushrooms

NOTE:
Sometimes I add a little Italian salad dressing for extra flavor...
(don't use too much!)

Cucumber Salad

3 cukes
herb salt
dill weed
tamari
sour cream
onion (optional)
chives (optional)
} to taste

Peel and slice the cukes and put in a serving dish. Sprinkle with tamari, herb salt & dill. Add several tablespoons of sour cream. Chop up the onion and mix in.

Chill an hour before serving.

Nancy's Tabouleh

— a terrific summer salad

1 cup bulghur (a grain – ask for at health food stores)
1 cup boiling water
1 cucumber – peeled, seeded & chopped
4 minced fresh tomatoes
1½ cups chopped fresh parsley
½ cup chopped scallions
½ cup fresh mint leaves (or 1 tbsp. dried) (optional)
½ cup olive oil
⅓ cup lemon juice
½ tsp. salt
¼ tsp. pepper
1 tsp. tamari

Boil water and pour over bulghur in a bowl. Let sit 10 minutes – drain excess water out (squeeze with hands). Prepare vegetables and add to bulghur Add remaining ingredients and toss.
Chill and serve.

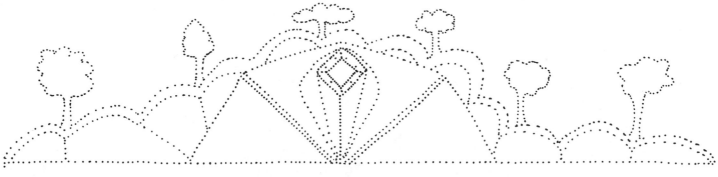

Italian Tomato & Pepper Salad

when it's hot and tomatoes are overly abundant... try this as an alternative to a green salad.

5 large fresh tomatoes, cut in rounds or into bite-size cubes

2 green peppers, prepare same as tomatoes

¼ cup olive oil

2 tbsp. lemon juice

2 tbsp. wine vinegar

2 garlic cloves, pressed

½ tsp. oregano

½ tsp. basil

Salt & pepper to taste

Prepare tomatoes and peppers ~ place in a bowl. Mix the remaining ingredients together... pour over tomatoes & peppers, and marinate in refrigerator a few hours.

Mushroom Salad

⌐ this is a light salad to serve
when the main course is rich & filling.

1 lb. very fresh small mushrooms

½ cup olive oil

¼ cup vinegar

herb salt

tamari, to taste

Wash mushrooms well and slice.
Marinade them with the oil, vinegar,
salt and tamari. Toss and chill
for an hour.

... Can be served alone or placed
on top of some bib lettuce.

Guacamole

Guacamole is great as a dip with chips or with cut-up vegetables. I also like serving it as a salad on a generous portion of Romaine or Boston lettuce.

2 medium to large ripe avocadoes, mashed
1 tomato
½ red Bermuda onion
2 large cloves garlic, crushed
juice of 1 lemon
1 or 2 hot chilis   (you can find these in a jar in the Mexican food section of supermarkets)
herb or regular salt

In a bowl, place peeled and mashed avocado (leave a little chunky). Chop tomatoes & onion, and add to avocado — then add crushed garlic and chopped chilies (seeds and all). Squeeze in lemon and add herb salt. Mix well and chill. If serving as salad, place a heaping portion on top of lettuce and serve individually.

Spinach Salad

... fresh spinach right from the
garden is ~~too~~ good to cook ⌐ makes
a wonderful salad.

1 lb. fresh spinach (wash real well ⌐ wrap in a
cloth towel and refrigerate
while preparing rest of salad)
1 small red Bermuda onion ⌐ sliced in rings
2 hard boiled eggs, mashed
½ lb. fresh mushrooms, sliced
1 large carrot, grated
⌐ a little feta cheese is always a nice addition,
and some tofu croutons (see pg. 52)

Prepare all vegetables and toss with spinach.

Garnish with hard boiled eggs.

Dressing:

juice of 1 lemon

¼ cup olive oil

herb salt & pepper

pinch of sugar ... and perhaps a dash of
prepared ~~Dijon~~ mustard

... Mix well.

Dress immediately before serving.

Potato, Chicken & Broccoli Salad

this is a good way to use up leftover chicken in the summer.

8 medium potatoes
2 cups cooked chicken, diced
1 medium head raw broccoli
½ cup fresh parsley, chopped
½ cup mayonnaise (add more if you like)
1 tsp. Dijon mustard
herb salt
salt & pepper } to taste

Scrub and wash potatoes (leave the skins on for just-the-right-touch!) Put in pot & cover with water. Bring to a boil and cook about ½ hour till tender, but not mushy. Drain and cool. Cut up into bite-size pieces —add cooked chicken and broccoli flowers. In a small bowl mix parsley, mayonnaise and mustard together. Spoon into potato mixture and toss until vegetables & chicken are well coated. Add salt and pepper to taste.

❦ Serve with sliced fresh tomatoes — sprinkled with basil.

The
Old Country Grated Rutabaga Salad

I was raised on this salad ~ it may sound strange, but try it... it's delicious and very good for you!

....

1 good sized rutabaga, peeled & coarsely grated

1 small onion, chopped

3 tbsp. oil

salt & pepper to taste

Grate rutabaga ~ leave coarse, as you don't want it to get mushy. Combine remaining ingredients and mix well.

Serve with a slice of rye bread!

Ilse's Spinach Pasta Salad
~ grand !

1 lb. spinach ribbon noodles
3 scallions, chopped
3 large fresh tomatoes, diced
1 red or green pepper (cut into long slivers)
½ cup chopped fresh parsley
4 oz. lightly roasted pine nuts
2 4-oz. jars marinated artichoke hearts
(liquid and all)
1 can pitted black olives, sliced
a few pitted green olives, sliced
1 cup freshly grated parmesan or
romano cheese
juice of 1 lemon
salt & pepper ⎫
tamari ⎬ to taste
a pinch of oregano or basil

Combine all ingredients (except pasta) in a bowl. Toss. Cook pasta ~ run under cold water. Drain well. Mix with other ingredients. Chill or serve at room temperature.

PASTA MAKES A GREAT SUMMER SALAD ~ there are many different types & shapes of pasta, and an endless amount of ingredients to add to them.

NOTE: I like to use spaghetti or linguini noodles sometimes and change Ilse's salad around ~ I use feta and parmesan cheese... raw zucchini is wonderful... carrots, celery, mushrooms, broccoli, cauliflower... use your imagination.

serves 8 to 10

Potato Salad

↳ a favorite at picnics!

8 to 10 medium potatoes (I like to use the red bliss potatoes — skins and all)
4 hard boiled eggs
½ cup chopped scallions
1 medium green pepper, chopped
¾ cup chopped celery
½ cup grated carrots
1 bunch fresh parsley, chopped
1 cup mayonnaise
salt & pepper to taste (herb salt preferred)
paprika on top before serving

Boil potatoes with skins... till cooked, but not mushy. Drain and cool. Prepare vegetables. Cut cooled potatoes into bite-size pieces. Chop up hard boiled eggs. Combine potatoes, eggs and vegies in bowl ↳ mix well... add mayo, parsley, herb salt (and/or salt) and pepper. Mix. Refrigerate a few hours.

Sprinkle with paprika before serving.

Creamy Guacamole

↳ a great dip that goes well with both crackers and vegie sticks

4 ripe avocados
1 cup of sour cream
2 large cloves garlic, pressed
4 tbsp. of hot sauce or salsa
juice of 1 lemon
herb salt to taste

Mash avocado ⌒ add lemon, garlic and herb salt to taste. Mix in sour cream and salsa.

Chill and serve.

> Melt a little cheese on bread or a bagel and spread some quacamole on top ⌒ add sprouts, tomato & onion... and you have a great luncheon sandwich.

Winter Vegetable Salad

this is a nice change from green salad in the winter...

Use as much as you wish of the following:

broccoli, cut into small flowers
Cauliflower, in small flowers
green or red peppers, cut into strips
scallions
carrots
celery
Jerusalem artichokes (delicious raw in salads - look for in supermarket)
potatoes, cooked and diced
zucchini, sliced small
parsley

Toss and serve on a bed of Romaine lettuce. This salad goes well with Mustard Vinaigrette Dressing

(see pg. 46)

··· ideas for enhancing *Fruit Salad*

some suggestions for different fruits :

strawberries ⎫ or any other
blueberries ⎭ berries in season
cantelope
honeydew melon
watermelon
crenshaw melon
seedless grapes
apples
oranges
pineapple
bananas

Kiwi fruit
mangos
papayas
raisins
dates
prunes
figs
walnuts ⎫ and other
almonds ⎭ nuts
coconut

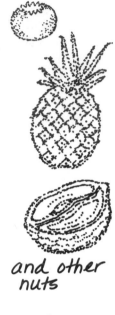

Prepare your fruit and mix together – add
bananas when ready to serve, to prevent
browning.
Mix in some sour cream, sweetened with
honey or maple syrup ⌣ or use a plain
yogurt or a fruit yogurt. A little fruit
liqueur is a wonderful addition ... I love
a rasberry liqueur called Chambord.

serves 4

Russian Delight

a refreshing <u>salad</u> to accompany
a light meal on a hot summers day.

   3 small-ish cucumbers, peeled & cubed
     (if you grow your own organic
       cukes — leave skins on)

   3 scallions, chopped

   3 radishes, chopped

   1 cup sour cream

   salt and pepper

Mix all the above ingredients together.
Chill and serve.

Great with fish and corn-on-the-cob.

Avocado Salad Dressing

1 avocado
½ cup sour cream
1 tbsp. oil
juice of 1 lemon
1 clove garlic, pressed
a pinch of dried parsley
herb salt & pepper to taste

Scoop out avocado — combine with remaining ingredients and blend well.

... a food processor or blender makes a creamy dressing — if blending by hand, mash avocado in a bowl and add other ingredients... beat with a wire whisk.

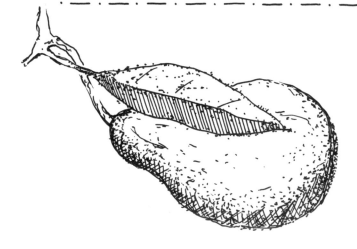
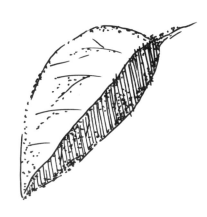

Italian Salad Dressing

2 cups olive oil
¾ cup apple cider vinegar
¼ cup tamari
2 large cloves garlic, (pressed)
¼ tsp. basil
¼ tsp. oregano
½ tsp. Dijon mustard
¼ cup grated parmesan cheese (optional)

Mix all ingredients in a bottle with a cap. Shake well before serving. Remove dressing from refrigerator at least ½ hour before using, as olive oil will solidify when cold.

Savory Roquefort or Bleu Cheese Dressing

½ cup mayonnaise
½ cup yogurt or sour cream
½ cup crumbled Roquefort or
                      Bleu Cheese
pinch of parsley

Mix together thoroughly. Serve with freshly ground pepper.

Mustard Vinaigrette Dressing

When I make dressing, I usually like to make enough to last, as it will keep in the refrigerator for weeks... getting better as it ages. Find a cruet or bottle with tight lid to store.

1 cup olive oil
½ cup vinegar (wine or apple cider vinegar)

1 clove garlic, pressed
3 tbsp. Dijon mustard
4 tsp. basil
salt & pepper or herb salt

Place the ingredients in jar. Cover and shake well. This is a good dressing to use on the Winter Vegetable Salad
(see pg. 41)

Anne's Tahini-Garlic Salad Dressing

~ great!

makes a large batch... Keeps in
                refrigerator forever!

½ cup safflower oil ⎫ or use 1 cup of
½ cup olive oil ⎬ one or the other
¾ cup apple cider vinegar (or any other)
½ cup tamari or soya sauce
½ cup sesame tahini (see pg. 237)
3 cloves crushed garlic
½ tsp. oregano
½ tsp. basil

Mix in jar ~ shake well. Use on
salad as desired.

"Lo-Cal" Yogurt Salad Dressing

1 pint plain yogurt

1 medium bunch fresh washed parsley

1 or 2 cloves garlic, crushed

salt or Herbamare to taste
(see pg. 234)

Combine the above in blender &
whirl till garlic is incorporated.

French Dressing

... serve hot or cold

1 cup tomato sauce
¼ cup honey
¼ cup vinegar
1 clove garlic, pressed
a pinch of basil
a pinch of tarragon
salt & pepper
½ cup Bleu Cheese, crumbled

Put all ingredients, except for Bleu Cheese in a saucepan and bring to a boil. Reduce heat and simmer 5 minutes. Remove from heat and let cool slightly... then add crumbled Blue Cheese. And serve over salad.

Sesame Tahini Salad Dressing

½ cup tahini (see pg.237)

½ cup water

juice of 1 lemon

1 large clove garlic, pressed

herb salt to taste

> this is an unusual salad dressing which is easy to make and stores well in the refrigerator

Place tahini in a jar. Add water and mix well. Add lemon, garlic and herb salt. Cover and shake well before serving.

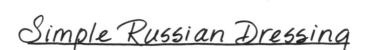

Simple Russian Dressing

1 cup mayonnaise

¼ cup Ketchup

1 tbsp. pickle relish

Mix and serve.

... that's about it really ⌣ if you want, add a little ground pepper and perhaps some chopped parsley.

Homemade Croutons

these croutons can transform a bowl of greens !

2 slices bread (homemade whole wheat is the best)
1 large clove garlic, pressed
2 tbsp. butter

Cut bread into large cubes ⌐ melt butter in a skillet. Add pressed garlic, then bread ... and sauté till bread is golden and crispy. Serve.

... try adding a few to a bowl of soup!

Caroline's
...Tofu Croutons...

... a wonderful addition to a green salad — with a little cheese & crackers you can have a nice light summer meal.

2 cakes tofu (1 lb.)
1 large clove fresh garlic, pressed
¼ cup pine nuts
¼ cup sunflower seeds
¼ cup sesame seeds
tamari to taste
2 tbsp. oil

Pat tofu dry with paper towel — cut into small cubes and set aside. In a skillet, place all the nuts and seeds, and brown well. Remove seeds. In same skillet, heat oil till hot... put tofu and garlic in and brown <u>real</u> well. Add roasted seeds. Sprinkle in tamari. Mix well. Let cool and toss with salad.

Breads

Potato Bread or Rolls

...the potatoes give this bread a wonderful
flavor and a good slicing consistency.

7 to 8 cups flour (½ unbleached white & ½ whole wheat is good)
1 cup mashed potatoes (only fresh will do)
1½ cups warm water
3 pkg. or tbsp. dry yeast
3 tbsp. honey or sugar
1 tbsp. salt
2 eggs
1 stick butter or margarine

for top { 1 egg, beaten
sesame seeds or poppy seeds

Wash and peel about 3 large potatoes ⌐ cut up and put in pot...
cover with water and cook till soft. Drain & mash ⌐ set aside.
In warm water, dissolve yeast & honey and let rest 10 min. till
bubbly. In a large mixing bowl, place 2 cups flour, 2 eggs,
stick of softened butter, warm mashed potatoes and yeast
mixture. Beat well with a wooden spoon or an electric mixer
till well blended ⌐ a few minutes. Add remaining flour gradually.
Continue to beat until the dough becomes too stiff to beat with
a spoon or mixer. Then remove the dough to a floured board
and knead while continuing to add the remaining flour. Knead
till satiny smooth ⌐ if sticky, add a little more flour. Place in
oiled bowl & let rise 1 hr. or till double. Punch down. Form into
2 loaves & place into greased loaf pans or form into rolls and
place on greased cookie sheets. Brush with egg & sprinkle on
seeds.
Bake loaves 45 to 55 min. or till golden ⌐ at 375°.
Bake rolls 15 to 20 min. or till golden ⌐ at 375°

Serve
Warm!

Robust Rye Bread

makes 2 loaves

2 pkg. (or 2 tbsp.) dry yeast
1½ cups lukewarm water
1½ cups lukewarm milk
¼ cup honey
4 tsp. salt
½ cup oil
2 tbsp. caraway seeds
4 cups rye flour
3 cups whole wheat flour
3 cups unbleached white flour
1 egg ~ well beaten for crust

Dissolve yeast in warm water and add honey ~ let sit 10 min. In another bowl mix salt, oil & seeds. Add bubbling yeast mixture ~ blend in rye flour and enough whole wheat and unbleached white flour to make a stiff dough. Knead till satiny smooth, adding flour as you go (5 to 10 min.) Put in oiled bowl ~ cover and let rise till double. Punch down. Divide into 2 balls and form into loaves. Place on oiled cookie sheet. Let rise till double. Brush with egg. Bake at 375° for 35 to 40 minutes. Cool well before cutting.

Delicious... great sandwich bread!

Tracey's Italian Bread

This recipe comes straight from Italy! Dough can also be used for pizza or pumpushkies... see bottom of page.

8 to 9 cups unbleached white flour
2 tsp. salt
2 tbsp. dry yeast
2½ cups lukewarm water
olive oil

In a small bowl, sprinkle yeast over lukewarm water - let stand 10 min. In a large bowl, mix 7 c. of flour together with salt and form a well in the middle for the liquids. Pour yeast mixture into well and gradually blend together - as flour is incorporated and dough stiffens, begin kneading, adding remaining flour as necessary to get a tight firm dough. Knead until smooth & elastic (oil your hands w/ olive oil while kneading). Place dough in a well oiled bowl - cover w/ a towel and sit in a draft-free spot - let rise till doubled (about 1½ to 2 hrs.) Punch down & knead 5 to 10 min. Let rest 10 min. Form into 2 loaves - place on oiled baking sheet & let rise till double. Make a couple slits in each loaf w/ a sharp knife and bake at 400° for 45 minutes. (When done, bread will make a dull thump when knocked on bottom.)

Pizza - makes 2 large pizza crusts

Sprinkle cornmeal on pizza pans or cookie sheets - roll dough out - top with whatever you like and bake in a <u>hot</u> 500° oven for 20 minutes or so.

Pumpushkies -

After first rising and second kneading, pull off walnut-sized pieces of dough - flatten in your hand and stretch... pull a hole in the center and deep fry. Drain on paper towels and while hot, sprinkle with sugar, cinnamon or other stickable toppings. They're also great <u>plain</u> with hot soup.

Challah
～ Braided Egg Bread ～

... makes 1 very large loaf ～ or 2 good-sized ones. Great holiday bread
... <u>very</u> special!

<u>Combine</u>: 1 cup warm water
2 pkg. active dry yeast (or 2 tbsp.)
2 tsp. honey

～ Let sit 5 to 10 minutes.

<u>Add to above</u>: 3 eggs, plus 1 egg white (reserve yolk for crust)
5 tbsp. oil
1½ tbsp. salt
1 tsp. honey
4 cups mixture of unbleached white & ww flour...(or all of one or the other, as you prefer)
plus <u>1 cup</u> for kneading

(poppy or sesame seeds (optional))

～ Beat well as you add flour till stiff.

Then... Knead, and let rise in oiled, covered bowl till double. Punch down. Separate and roll into three coils (for 1 loaf) or 6 coils (for 2 loaves). Start off by pinching the ends together, and then braid as you would hair. Place on greased cookie sheet (or sheets... it's huge!) and cover with a towel. Let rise till double. Brush with egg yolk. Sprinkle with poppy or sesame seeds. Bake in preheated oven at 425° for 15 minutes. Reduce to 350° and bake for 30 minutes or until golden. Keep your eye on it, 'cause it cooks fast.

·57·

Lizzy's Deliciously Wholesome

Whole Wheat Bread

and

* Cinnamon Buns

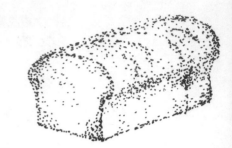

12 (±) cups whole wheat flour
4 cups warm milk
4 tbsp. baking yeast
½ cup warm water
3 tbsp. salt
6 tbsp. oil
1 cup honey
¼ cup nutritional yeast
¼ cup wheat germ

Dissolve yeast in warm water, adding about 1 tsp. honey. Set aside. Heat milk. Combine salt, oil and warm milk. Add honey and blend well. Add nutritional yeast and wheat germ. Begin adding flour a cup at a time until a runny dough is formed. Add softened yeast. Stir well & continue adding flour until dough comes away from sides of bowl. Turn out on floured board and knead for about 10 minutes, adding some flour until dough is no longer sticky. Place dough back in oiled bowl (spin around & flip over, so the top gets oiled, too). Set in warm place to rise. When doubled in bulk, punch down & knead again for 5 to 10 minutes. Divide into 4 quarters. Place in oiled bread pans and let rise again (slightly) ⌐ letting it increase in size by about a third. Tops can then be brushed with beaten egg if desired. Bake in 350° oven for about an hour till well browned.

... Makes a beautiful braided bread, too!

* ... also makes great Cinnamon Buns :

After the first rise, roll dough flat ⌐ brush on some honey, melted butter & cinnamon mixture (to taste)... generously sprinkle on chopped walnuts and raisins. Roll dough like a jelly roll and slice in about $\frac{3}{4}$" slices. Place, touching each other, in oiled cake pan ⌐ and brush generously again with butter-honey-cinnamon mixture. Let rise again... then bake at 350° for about 45 minutes.

"I usually divide bread dough in quarters ... I like to make 3 loaves of bread & 1 batch of cinnamon buns (with the 4th quarter)"

Barbie's Gram's Oatmeal Bread

old fashioned and delicious !

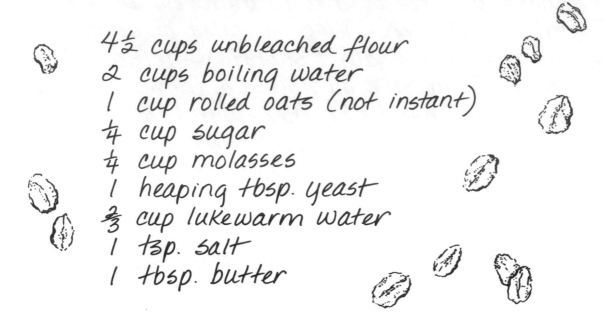

4½ cups unbleached flour
2 cups boiling water
1 cup rolled oats (not instant)
¼ cup sugar
¼ cup molasses
1 heaping tbsp. yeast
⅔ cup lukewarm water
1 tsp. salt
1 tbsp. butter

Combine yeast with ⅔ c. lukewarm water and let sit. Bring 2 c. water to a boil. Place oats, sugar, butter & salt in a large bowl ⌐ pour boiling water on top ... mix a minute and let stand, until lukewarm. When lukewarm, add the yeast mixture ⌐ mix and then begin adding flour, mixing well after each addition. When dough sticks together, take out of bowl and knead in remaining flour. Wash bowl and dry ⌐ put in about 1 tsp. oil and place dough in ... flip around to coat dough with oil. Cover & let rise till double. Split dough in half ⌐ place into 2 oiled bread pans. Let rise again (1 hr.). Bake in 400° oven for 40 to 45 minutes.

Nut Bread

a quick, slightly sweet bread
... good for a brunch or tea ⌣

1 cup whole wheat flour
1 cup unbleached white flour
2 eggs
2 tsp. baking powder
½ tsp. salt
1 cup milk or buttermilk
½ cup honey
5 tbsp. melted butter
1 cup chopped walnuts

Preheat oven to 350°. Oil a large bread pan or a flat Pyrex dish.

Sift your dry ingredients. Beat the remaining ingredients. Mix with dry ingredients. Blend well but don't overbeat.

Spoon into bread pan or Pyrex dish. Bake loaf pan 45 minutes at 350°, or till cake tester comes out clean. Bake Pyrex dish about ½ hour.

Serve warm or cool with butter! Cream Cheese and jam are delightful accompaniments as well.

Blueberry Muffins

~ great with breakfast or lunch!

1 cup whole wheat flour
1 cup unbleached white flour
2 tsp. baking powder
1 cup milk or buttermilk
2 eggs, beaten
4 tbsp. salted butter, melted
3 tbsp. maple syrup or honey
1 tsp. vanilla
1 cup blueberries
a pinch of salt

Preheat oven to 375°. Butter a 12-cup muffin tin. Sift dry ingredients. Beat eggs, milk, butter, vanilla and maple syrup or honey together. Add to dry ingredients ~ add blueberries. Mix. Spoon into muffin tin and bake 25 to 30 minutes or till golden.

Serve warm or at room temperature.

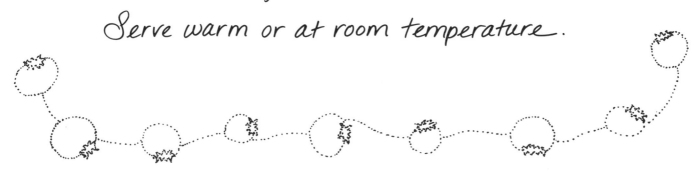

Dianne's {Good} Biscuits

1¾ cup whole wheat flour (or unbleached white or combination of both)
¼ cup wheat germ
4 tsp. baking powder
½ tsp. cream of tartar
pinch of salt
½ cup shortening, butter or margarine
2 tsp. honey
⅔ cup milk (enriched with 3 tbsp. of non-fat dry milk — optional)

Sift flour, salt, baking powder, cream of tartar and wheat germ into bowl. Cut in shortening and honey until mixture looks like coarse crumbs. Add milk all at once and stir until dough follows fork around bowl. Pat or roll dough ½" thick. Cut with biscuit cutter.

Bake on ungreased cookie sheet in hot oven — 400° — for 10 to 12 minutes.

Barbara's Zucchini Bread

3 eggs
1 cup oil
1 cup sugar
2 cups grated & well drained zucchini, unpeeled
2 tsp. vanilla
2½ cups flour
1 tsp. baking powder
2 tsp. baking soda
2 tsp. cinnamon
½ tsp. ground ginger
½ tsp. nutmeg
¾ tsp. salt
1 cup raisins (optional)
1 cup chopped nuts

Beat eggs slightly in large bowl. Stir in oil, sugar, zucchini and vanilla. Sift flour, baking powder, baking soda, cinnamon and salt. Add to egg mixture and blend well. Stir in nuts, and raisins (if desired). Spoon batter into two well-greased loaf pans.

Bake at 350° for 1 hour. Cool in pans 10 min., then remove from pans and cool completely.

Banana Bread

I made this one morning very quickly, as
I had some bananas that needed to be
used ⌣ and it turned out great!

3 cups flour
2 cups mashed ripe bananas
1 cup maple syrup or honey
1 stick melted butter
3 eggs, beaten
½ cup raisins
1 tsp. vanilla
1 tsp. cinnamon
¼ tsp. mace
⅛ tsp. nutmeg
1 tsp. grated lemon or orange rind
(optional)

2 heaping tbsp. baking powder
pinch of salt

Combine all of the above ingredients in a large
bowl and mix well with a wooden spoon. Spoon
into 2 greased bread pans and bake for
1 hour at 350°.

Serve warm or cooled ⌣ plain, with butter,
cream cheese or jam.

Lee & Linda's Grannies Date-Nut Bread

1 8-oz. pkg. pitted dates
1½ cups boiling water
2 tsp. baking soda
¼ tsp. salt
2½ cups flour
1 tsp. baking powder
1 cup sugar
2 tbsp. butter
1 beaten egg
1 tsp. vanilla
1 full cup chopped walnuts
1 mashed ripe banana (for moistness, if desired ~ optional)

Cut dates in quarters ~ put in bowl of boiling water with baking soda and butter, and let cool. Mix together flour, baking powder, salt, sugar and beaten egg. Mix into date mixture. Add walnuts and blend real well. Spoon into two well greased bread pans. Bake at 325° for 1¼ to 1½ hours. Test center ~ don't overbake.
Serve warm or at room temperature with lots of butter!

Profound Pizza Dough

our compliments to Pat, wherever she is...
(last we heard, into wheat farming some-
where in the mid-west)... one 'heckuva
                                    cook!

1 pkg. yeast (1 tbsp.)
2½ cups whole wheat flour
2½ cups unbleached white flour
1 tsp. salt
1½ cups warm water
olive oil

In a large bowl, dissolve yeast in ½ c. warm water; next mix in about 3 c. flour, 1 tsp. salt and ½ c. warm water — then stir in ½ c. more warm water and rest of flour. Knead until well blended, then place in large oiled bowl, turning it over to oil top. Set dough, covered with clean towel, in warm place until doubled in bulk — about 1 hour or so. When dough has doubled, punch down and divide in half. Spread on oiled pizza pans or cookie sheets. Pinch edges up and brush rims with oil (to prevent burning). Add favorite tomato sauce and what-ever extras (see pg. 113). Top with grated cheese 5 minutes before done.

Bake 25 minutes in preheated hot-450°-oven.

Breakfasts

Har's "Holes-In-One"
or
"Howdy Doody Eggs"

eggs
bread, sliced
butter
salt & pepper

loved by Kids
of all ages!

Take some butter and melt in a skillet.
Take a slice of bread ⌐ butter it on
one side and then cut a hole in the
middle (save the middle ⌐ it's a very
important part!). Take bread and
place in buttered hot skillet... buttered
side up. Break an egg into the hole
and fry 3 minutes on that side. Then
flip to buttered side and fry 3 more
minutes. Season with salt & pepper
and serve with the middle of bread.

Elize's Mexican Omelet

6 eggs, beaten
3 oz. can of chili peppers, chopped
1 small onion, diced
¼ lb. grated Gruyère or Jack cheese
2 tbsp. butter
salt & pepper

salsa ~ for the top

Sauté onion and peppers in 1 tbsp. butter
for 5 minutes or till onion is transparent.
Remove from pan and set aside. Beat eggs
...add salt & pepper to taste. Melt 1 tbsp.
of butter in the same pan you sautéed
your vegies in or use an omelet pan. Cook
eggs till set, but still moist on top. Sprinkle
on grated cheese and vegies... fold in half.

Serve ~ pass a bowl of salsa
around the table.

Jacques' French Bread·French Toast

8 slices of bread (French bread best!)
4 eggs, beaten
¼ cup milk
1 tsp. vanilla
¼ tsp. cinnamon
¼ tsp. nutmeg
butter

Beat eggs and milk together in a bowl large enough to fit bread slices into — add vanilla, cinnamon and nutmeg ... mix. Dip bread into egg mixture to cover bread completely. Melt a little butter in a skillet and place bread in — cook until golden browned on both sides.

Serve with maple syrup ... cream cheese and jam ... hot applesauce ...

Breakfast Standby

I'm convinced that ideas are just as important as recipes ~ here's one of our favorite breakfasts.

1 cup granola

1 fruit yogurt (apple, strawberry, blueberry, etc. ... try ones made w/ honey)

2 apples, chopped

2 bananas, sliced

a handful of raisins

a handful of almonds or walnuts

There it is ... mix it altogether and serve.

Lovely Linda's Omelet Con Ricotta Cheese

~ don't be fooled by the name ... just Linda's fancy ~
   the omelet is quite simple ♥♥

6 eggs, beaten
1 cup ricotta cheese
1 heaping tsp. fresh or dried chives
a dash of garlic powder (optional)
salt & pepper, or Herbamare (see pg. 234)
parsley ~ for garnish
2 tbsp. butter

Beat the eggs ~ add a little Herbamare. Melt butter in a skillet or omelet pan. Cook eggs till set but still moist on top. Mix ricotta with chives ~ spoon onto eggs. Flip the eggs in half. Garnish with chopped parsley.

To make a sweet omelet ~ skip the chives & garlic ... and add apricot or any other fruit jam to ricotta.

Scrambled Tofu

... a great high-protein breakfast, lunch
or dinner — sit down to a large bowl of
it and still feel slim & trim when finished !!

2 lbs. tofu, crumbled
1 medium zucchini, chopped
2 scallions or 1 small onion, chopped
1 small garlic clove, pressed (optional)
2 tbsp. butter
½ tsp. parsley
herb salt and/or tamari to taste
½ tsp. tumeric (adds yellow color & a subtle flavor)
grated cheese (optional)

In a skillet, melt 2 tbsp. butter. Add chopped
scallions, zucchini and parsley. Sauté 5 min.
Add crumbled tofu (use your hands — it feels
great !). Sauté 5 to 10 minutes. While
sautéing, add a little tumeric, herb salt
and/or tamari.
If you like cheese, you can add a little
grated cheddar or jack at the last minute.
Shut the fire off and cover the pan for a
minute or two — till cheese melts.

(I think it's great without the cheese, too)

Sunday Brunch Frittata

8 eggs
2 tbsp. milk or cream
4 potatoes, chopped small (skins & all)
    —Red Bliss preferred—
1 onion, chopped
1 green pepper, chopped
¼ lb. mushrooms, sliced (optional)
1 medium tomato, chopped
¼ lb. cheddar cheese
1 small clove garlic, pressed (optional)
1 tsp. dried parsley (optional)
salt & pepper to taste
2 tbsp. butter
2 tbsp. oil
paprika — for garnish (optional)

Prepare vegetables. In a large skillet, heat oil and add potatoes. Sauté for 7 min. — add onion, pepper, mushrooms, tomatoes, garlic, parsley and some salt & pepper. Sauté 5 minutes or till potatoes are tender and onion is transparent. Remove vegies from pan and set aside. Beat eggs with cream — add some salt & pepper. In same skillet, melt butter — add beaten eggs. Spoon vegies on top of eggs evenly. Sprinkle cheese on top. Cover & cook slowly till eggs are firm. Remove from pan and cut into wedges. Serve.

Ken's Banana Pancakes

... these pancakes are truly worth the effort!

2 cups whole wheat pastry flour <u>or</u>
    1 cup ww pastry & 1 cup unbleached white

4 eggs, separated

1 cup milk

1 cup pureed bananas (or even ½ c. bananas &
    and ½ c. puréed strawberries ⌐ or
    could use <u>all</u> puréed strawberries)

¼ cup maple syrup

1 tsp. vanilla ⎫
pinch of cinnamon ⎬ optional
              ⎭
oil ⌐ for cooking pancakes

butter & maple syrup

Separate eggs and beat whites till stiff. Refrigerate whites. Mix flour, egg yolks and milk together. Purée fruit and mix with flour mixture. Add vanilla and cinnamon. Mix well. Put oil in skillet and heat real well. Take about 1 cup batter and add about 4 heaping tablespoons of stiff egg whites. Fold in and make pancakes. Cook until golden. Do same with rest of batter and whites (1 c. batter & 4 tbsp. whites) till used up.

Ken says it's important to add whites in this manner ⌐ that's what makes them light & fluffy.

serves 4 to 6

Inspiring Italian Omelet

8 to 10 eggs, beaten
1 cup slivered or chopped onions
½ cup chopped green or red peppers
1 medium zucchini, chopped
2 fresh tomatoes, chopped
a few sprigs fresh parsley or 1 tsp. dried
½ tsp. dried basil or fresh if available
½ tsp. dried oregano
¼ lb. freshly grated Romano, parmesan
  (or any other sharp Italian cheese)
4 tbsp. butter
Salt & pepper to taste

Grate cheese and set aside. Chop and sauté vegetables in 2 tbsp. butter, for 5 minutes. Add herbs
and a little salt & pepper ⌐ sauté another 3 min.
or so. Remove from pan and set aside. Beat the
eggs... add a little salt & pepper. In same pan,
melt the remaining butter and pour the beaten
eggs in and cook till set but still moist. Sprinkle
cheese on top and over that, the sautéed vegetables.
Fold the omelet in half and serve.

<u>Caroline's light'n lovely Blueberry / Cottage Cheese</u>
<u>Pancakes</u>

2 cups small curd cottage cheese
3 tbsp. honey or maple syrup
7 eggs, separated
1½ cups whole wheat flour / unbleached white
1 tsp. cinnamon
dash of salt
1 tsp. vanilla
1 cup fresh blueberries (or frozen)

oil

Separate eggs. Stir cottage cheese, honey, egg yolks and vanilla together in a large bowl. Slowly add flour, cinnamon and salt. Add blueberries. Beat egg whites until stiff, and gently fold into batter. Heat oil in skillet and pour batter into skillet in small rounds ~ about 3 to 4" in diameter. Cook like you would any pancake. When done, serve with butter and maple syrup.

...a breakfast to remember !

Rena's Oatmeal

Here's another breakfast idea ~ when I asked Rena for a recipe, she said all she can make is good oatmeal ... so here it is! She may not be a great cook, but she sure can weave!!

- Oatmeal for how many you wish
- Chopped apple
- raisins
- nuts
- granola
- butter
- milk
- honey or maple syrup

Make oatmeal as directed ~ season with butter, milk and honey. Top with chopped apples, raisins, nuts and a little granola... or you can add the apples & raisins while the oatmeal is cooking.

Spring Asparagus Omelet

6 eggs
5 medium stalks of asparagus (steam 5 min.)
1 onion, chopped
a few sprigs fresh parsley, chopped (or 4 tsp. dried)
herb salt to taste
pinch of marjoram
pinch of basil
2 tbsp. butter
2 tbsp. milk

In a skillet, add 1 tbsp. butter and sauté onion and spices. Steam asparagus 5 min. (leftover from last night's ↳ even better!) Drain and chop into large pieces. Mix with sauteed onion and spices ↳ set aside a minute. Beat eggs and milk with a wire whisk. Heat rest of butter in skillet (do not let butter brown). Pour egg mixture into pan and cook slowly... until the omelet sets up (about   minutes). Place vegies on top and fold omelet in half.

Serve immediately ↳ topped with sour cream and chives... or a little grated cheese.

Sauces

Teriyaki Sauce

~ for Teriyaki Chicken, Shrimp,
Swordfish, Tofu or Vegetables

½ cup tamari or soya sauce
½ cup Dr. Bronner's Liquid Bouillon
(see pg. 233)
¼ cup White Tiger Tofu Sauce ~ optional
(see pg. 237)

2 cloves garlic, pressed
½ cup sherry (optional)
2 tbsp. Dijon mustard
½ tsp. freshly grated ginger

Mix all the above ingredients together
and use as a marinade.

NOTE If you can't locate the Dr. B's or Tofu
Sauce, then use all tamari ... but do
ask for the other 2 at your health
food store.

Béchamel Sauce

A BASIC WHITE SAUCE

1 stick of lightly salted butter
½ cup flour
3 cups milk
½ tsp. salt
pepper

In a pot melt butter ~ add flour,
stir to make a roux. Add milk.
Cook over low heat, stirring constantly. Add salt and pepper.
Cook till thickens, stirring constantly.

POSSIBILITIES TO ADD, TO CHANGE SAUCE :
...mustard, horseradish, sautéed vegetables,
cheese & herbs

Spaghetti Sauce

⌐ *as we see it !*

1 lg. (28 oz.) can of crushed Italian tomatoes ⎫
2 lg. (28 oz. each) cans of tomato sauce　　　 ⎬ or *fresh* !
1 lg. (28 oz.) can of tomato puree　　　　　　⎭
1 12-oz. can of tomato paste
2 onions, chopped
1 green pepper, chopped
4 large cloves garlic, pressed
fresh parsley (or 1½ tsp. dried)
fresh basil (or 1 tsp. dried)
1 tbsp. oregano
1 bay leaf
½ cup red or white wine
¼ cup olive oil
3 tbsp. butter
salt & freshly ground pepper
2 tbsp. honey or sugar

NOTE: The best sauces are made with fresh, home-grown tomatoes... see opposite page —

In a large heavy pot, heat butter and oil ⌐ add onion, pepper, garlic and spices... and sauté 10 minutes. Add remaining ingredients, and simmer 2 hours or longer. Serve with a sharp Italian cheese (Locatella is excellent ⌐ take time to grate it yourself... it's worth it !)

The best tomato sauces are made from scratch... from home-grown tomatoes — if you ever get the chance, try it... it's really very rewarding. Putting up tomatoes in jars is fun — saves money, good for ecology, they look beautiful sitting on shelves, and they also make nice presents. When using fresh tomatoes, simply take as many ripe tomatoes as you want to use... put them into a pot of boiling water until the skins split... then drain and let cool. Peel skins off and squish up into a pot (go ahead — use your hands... it's really easier and feels great!) Simmer for hours — the longer the better — it thickens as it cooks. If you want a thicker sauce yet, add a can of tomato paste.

... You can use this for any tomato-based recipe — for example, spaghetti sauce, stewed tomatoes, and so on.

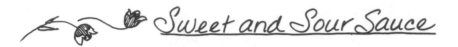

Sweet and Sour Sauce

... this is a wonderful, pungent sauce that is good on fish (see Sweet and Sour Shrimp~ pg.158), chicken, tofu or vegetables.

Sauce ~

1 16 oz. can of crushed or cubed
    pineapple, with juice
½ cup tomato sauce or ketchup
a little ginger
1 clove garlic, pressed
a dash of tamari
1 tbsp. cornstarch or arrowroot
            flour

In a saucepan place all ingredients, except cornstarch. Bring to a low boil, then add corn-starch, and lower flame. Stir constantly for about 5 minutes... till it thickens slightly.

Denise's Delicate Mushroom Sauce

...this is good served on brown rice

½ lb. mushrooms
3 scallions
3 tbsp. butter or margarine
¼ tsp. basil
½ tsp. parsley (or 3 sprigs of fresh)
¼ cup flour
½ cup milk
½ cup water
1 tbsp. Dijon mustard
herb salt or salt & pepper, to taste

Wash and chop mushrooms and scallions. Place in pan with butter and sauté 5 minutes. Add basil, parsley & herb salt— then flour, and stir well to make a roux. To that, add water, milk & mustard. Heat 5 minutes. Stir well and serve over brown rice ..... with steamed broccoli and a salad ... for a light, yet satisfying meal.

Tahini - Miso Sauce

...for chicken, tofu, rice & vegies...

½ cup tahini (see pg. 237)
¼ cup miso (see pg. 234)
½ cup water

Place all ingredients in a small pot
and heat, stirring constantly to
incorporate lumps.

a mild <u>or</u> hot <u>Curry Sauce</u>

... good on fish, vegetables, tofu ~
even on a green salad ...

    2 cups sour cream or yogurt
    4 tbsp. butter
    2 cloves garlic, pressed
    1 tsp. ground curry powder
    ½ tsp. tumeric   (or... use more or less)
    ¼ tsp. cumin
    ¼ tsp. cardamom
    ¼ tsp. coriander

In a saucepan melt butter ~ add
garlic and spices. Mix well & simmer
a minute or two. Add sour cream.
Stir and heat ~ about 5 minutes.

a small amount
of chopped onion
<u>and</u> apple can be
added with the
garlic, for an
unusual touch.

Denise's Onion Gravy or Sauce

... nice over rice

5 tbsp. butter or oil
1 onion, sliced
2 tbsp. grated carrot
1 small bay leaf
4½ tbsp. arrowroot flour
       (or cornstarch)
2 cups water (add a vegie bouillon cube if you like)
herb salt

Heat oil — add onion, bay leaf & carrot...
sauté 5 minutes. Add arrowroot to
½ cup bouillon to make a thin paste.
Add remaining stock to vegies in the
pan. Bring to a low boil. Gradually
stir in arrowroot mixture. Turn down
heat immediately. Cook, simmering till
thick and smooth.

Pesto

Pesto is a wonderful and easy sauce
for pasta, vegetables or fish ... it
must be made with fresh basil.

1 large bunch of basil (approx. 2 packed cups)
2 large cloves garlic, pressed
1 cup pine nuts
½ lb. sharp Italian cheese (Fontina, Parmesan, Romano, Locatella)
small bunch fresh parsley
4 tbsp. olive oil
4 tbsp. butter

Melt butter in a pan. Add olive oil. In a
food processor or blender, whirl basil,
garlic, nuts, cheese and parsley. Pour in
butter and oil. Blend well. Mix with
fresh cooked and drained pasta.
Serve immediately.

Barbecue Sauce

... for tofu, fish or chicken

1 8-oz. can of tomato sauce
3 tbsp. honey
2 tbsp. apple cider vinegar
1 tbsp. Worcestershire Sauce
1 tbsp. soya sauce or tamari
1 tbsp. prepared mustard
1 clove garlic, pressed
2 tbsp. minced onion (optional)
¼ tsp. cayenne pepper (optional)
  salt & pepper to taste

Combine all the above ingredients and mix well.

Vanilla Sauce

2 cups milk
2 egg yolks
½ cup honey
2 tsp. vanilla
2 tbsp. arrowroot
    flour

> This is a basic vanilla sauce... if you would like to vary, try adding fruit liqueurs (2 tbsp.). There's a delightful rasberry liqueur called Chambord; also, there are orange and coffee liqueurs.

In a medium saucepan place milk, honey and vanilla. Heat on low flame (do not boil). Add arrowroot and stir in well. Beat egg yolks ~ take about ½ cup hot milk mixture and add to egg yolks (to adjust heat... to prevent eggs from curdling). Mix well. Add to pot. Stir a couple minutes till sauce thickens slightly.

Serve hot on fruit pies or on
               apple cobbler ~

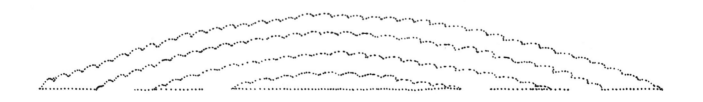

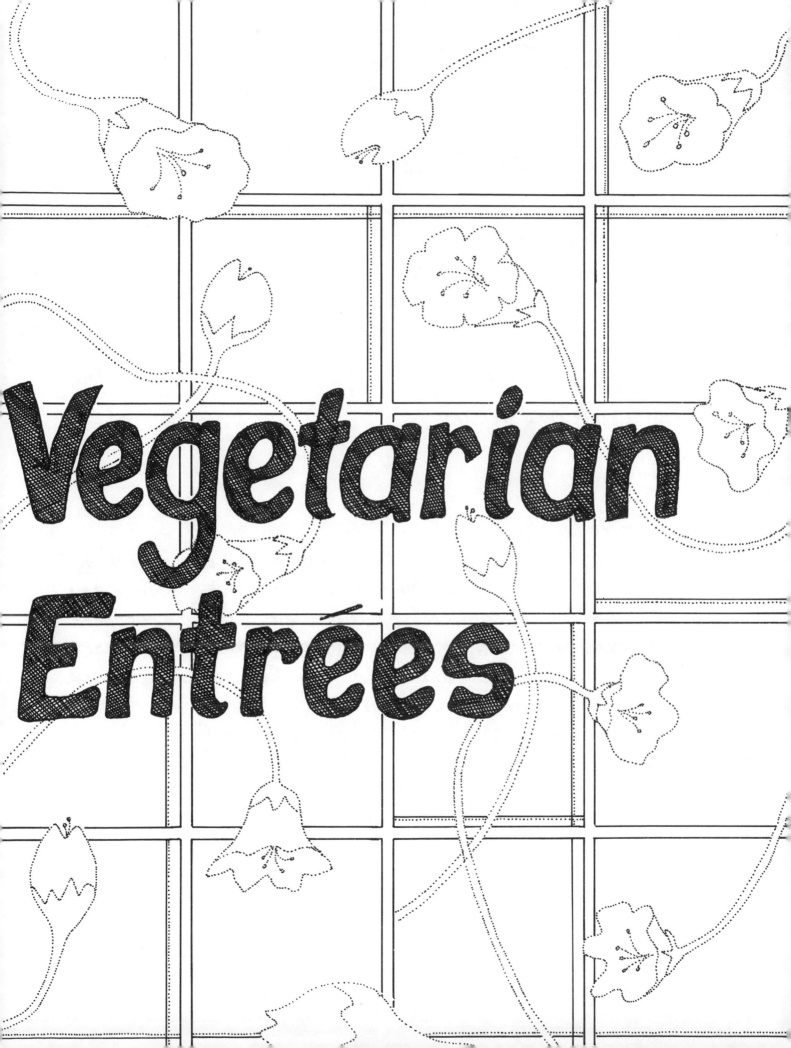

Vegetarian Entrées

Spinach Pie

Crust for 1 pie (see pg. 231)

....

1 lb. fresh chopped spinach (or frozen)
1 onion, chopped
1 lg. clove garlic, pressed
½ lb. sliced mushrooms (optional)
1 tbsp. fresh or dried parsley
½ tsp. fresh or dried basil
herb salt to taste
freshly ground pepper
1 tbsp. butter

White Sauce:

2 eggs
4 tbsp. butter
2 cups milk
¼ cup flour
herb salt to taste

....

5 oz. grated cheddar cheese

Make crust.

Wash spinach well — steam a few minutes and drain real well. In a skillet, melt 1 tbsp. butter and sauté for 5 minutes: onion, garlic, mushrooms, parsley, basil, salt and pepper. In medium pot, melt 4 tbsp. butter — remove from heat and stir in ¼ cup flour to make a roux. Replace on heat and gradually add milk (2 cups) and salt & pepper to taste. Stir constantly and bring to a boil. Reduce heat and add cheese — stir till cheese melts. Beat eggs lightly and mix in. Add sautéed vegetables and spinach — mix all together well. Spoon into pie crust and bake 45 minutes at 350° or till golden and firm.

Ruthie's South-of-the-Border Cauliflower Rellenos

Rellenos

1 lg. cauliflower
½ to ¾ lb. mild or sharp cheddar cheese
1 cup bread crumbs
2 eggs, beaten
herb salt
pinch of cumin (optional)
oil

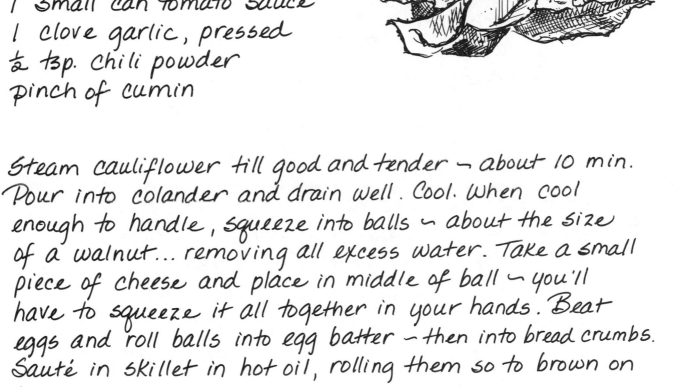

Sauce

1 small can tomato sauce
1 clove garlic, pressed
½ tsp. chili powder
pinch of cumin

Steam cauliflower till good and tender — about 10 min.
Pour into colander and drain well. Cool. When cool
enough to handle, squeeze into balls — about the size
of a walnut... removing all excess water. Take a small
piece of cheese and place in middle of ball — you'll
have to squeeze it all together in your hands. Beat
eggs and roll balls into egg batter — then into bread crumbs.
Sauté in skillet in hot oil, rolling them so to brown on
both sides.
To make sauce — put all ingredients in a pot and simmer
15 min. or so. You can either put balls into sauce or pour
sauce over balls.
 Serve hot with buttered noodles and a salad.

Brown Rice Stuffing

... for roasted chicken or turkey

3 cups cooked brown rice

1 large clove garlic, pressed

1 onion, sliced small

½ lb. mushrooms, sliced

1 stalk celery, chopped

1 carrot, grated

⅔ cup pine nuts

½ cup chopped fresh parsley (or 1 tsp. dried)

2 tbsp. butter

herb salt ⎫
tamari ⎬ to taste

freshly ground pepper (optional)

½ tsp. poultry seasoning — or a sprinkle of thyme, sage and rosemary

Cook rice as directed. In a skillet, melt butter — sauté garlic, onion, mushrooms, celery, grated carrot 5 minutes or so. Add pine nuts and parsley. Mix with rice and season well. Stuff into a chicken or turkey, and roast... basting frequently.

See Sheryl's Dynamite Chicken recipe (pg. 183) for a good way to prepare chicken or turkey.

Tofu Crusted Pizza

...different... not too fattening —
  high in protein and very tasty

3 lbs. tofu, sliced thin
3 cups tomato sauce (see pg. 86)
½ lb. mozzarella or jack cheese

pizza toppings (see pg. 113)
butter or oil

Cut each block of tofu into thin slices and
sauté in a skillet, in butter or oil (or
combination of both) till tofu is good and
crispy. Place on pizza pan or cookie sheet.
Cover with sauce, cheese and whatever
else you like. Bake at 400° for 30 to 40
minutes.

You will need a fork for this pizza!

Barbie's Ricotta Eggplant Parmesan

↳ al la paper towels!

1½ to 2 quarts tomato sauce (see pg. 86)
2 large eggplants, sliced
2 lbs. ricotta cheese
1 lb. mozzarella cheese, cut in chunks
1 cup parmesan cheese
2 cups bread or cracker crumbs
3 eggs, beaten
½ cup milk
1 tbsp. paprika

safflower oil
salt

Peel and slice eggplant into ¼" rounds - lay slices on paper towels (don't stack) - sprinkle each slice with salt & allow to sit for 15 min. (Eggplant will sweat... pat off excess water with more paper towels, turn slices over and repeat). Beat eggs and milk. Mix paprika with bread crumbs. Place eggplant slices in egg batter, then into bread crumbs... sauté till lightly golden on both sides. Drain on paper towels. Repeat till all eggplant is used. In a large 9x13 casserole, pour in enough tomato sauce to cover bottom - put in a layer of eggplant - dab with ricotta - place some mozzarella on top - sprinkle with parmesan - then some sauce - and continue to layer till ingredients are all used up, except the parmesan. Top with sauce. Sprinkle with remaining parmesan cheese and bake at 350° for 40 minutes, till bubbly.

Fettucini Prima Vera

this dish is best made when tomatoes are in season ↝ magnificant!

1½ lbs. fettucini noodles (do check out artichoke pasta... see pg. 236)

6 good-sized fresh tomatoes, chopped

5 <u>large</u> cloves garlic, pressed

a handful of fresh parsley, chopped

2 small or 1 med. zucchini, diced

1 head broccoli <u>stalks</u>, chopped (save the flower-tops for something else)

1 cup fresh peas

8 oz. fresh parmesan or romano cheese, grated

1 stick butter

¼ cup dry white or red wine

a pinch of oregano and basil

salt & pepper to taste

Put water up to boil for cooking pasta. Meanwhile, chop tomatoes ↝ take ½ of them and put in a skillet with the butter and garlic ↝ sauté 5 minutes. Add basil, oregano & parsley... sauté 5 more minutes. Add wine and cheese. Simmer till cheese melts. Add the broccoli, zucchini, peas and the remaining chopped tomatoes. Season with salt and pepper. Stir and remove from heat. At this point, the noodles <u>should be cooked</u> already. Drain. Place in a serving bowl and pour sauce on top. Toss well and <u>serve immediately</u>.

serves 4 to 6

<u>Tofu Shish Kebobs</u> or just <u>Barbecued Tofu</u>

...Tofu is great barbecued on wood or charcoal

Barbecue Sauce (see pg. 94) or
                        Teriyaki Sauce (see pg. 84)

2 lbs. tofu
2 green peppers
2 large sweet Spanish onions
1 lb. large fresh mushrooms
2 to 3 large fresh tomatoes

wooden or metal skewers
        and basting brush

Make barbecue or teriyaki sauce as directed. Cut tofu and vegetables into large cubes - place in a large bowl (handle carefully to keep tofu and vegies intact). Pour sauce over all and refrigerate as long as possible. Alternate tofu and vegies on individual skewers and place on grill over hot charcoal or wood (wood fires are nice - then you don't have to use lighter fluid). Turn and baste frequently. It's finished when the peppers and onions are browned and soft.

Serve over brown rice.

Cindi's Ratatouille Pie

Pie Crust ~ see pg. 231

Ratatouille prepared as below :

1 med. zucchini, cut in ¼" slices
1 cup peeled & diced eggplant
1 med. green pepper, thinly sliced
1 med. onion, sliced
2 chopped tomatoes, skinned & seeds removed
½ small hot pepper, very thinly sliced (optional)
2 garlic cloves, diced
⅓ cup fresh chopped parsley
1 whole bay leaf
1 tsp. basil
½ tsp. thyme
½ tsp. oregano
salt & pepper as desired
oil
¼ to ½ lb. mozzarella

Sauté in oil - zucchini & eggplant in large fry pan till lightly browned. Remove & drain on paper towels. In same pan, sauté parsley, peppers, onions & tomatoes just until tender. In saucepan combine zucchini & eggplant and vegetable mixture w/ spices. Cover & simmer slowly, about 45 min. Cool. (* can be prepared ahead & frozen, if desired)

Bake pie shell as directed until just golden ~ cool. Sprinkle ½ cup cheese on bottom of cooled pie crust. Fill pie shell w/ well-drained ratatouille (save any leftovers for a cold dip w/ crackers). Sprinkle remaining mozzarella on top of pie. Bake at 350° for ½ hour or until cheese is golden brown. Let sit 10 minutes before slicing.

Birdie's Vegie Burgers

Great on a roll with lettuce, tomatoes & the works!
Or serve without a roll, accompanied by a salad and a vegetable.

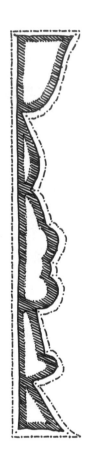

2 cups rolled oats
1½ cups grated carrots
½ cup diced string beans
½ cup diced cabbage
½ cup diced broccoli
½ cup diced mushrooms
½ cup diced onions
1 clove garlic, pressed
3 tbsp. flour (give or take a little)
¼ cup water
¼ cup tamari
salt & pepper to taste
oil
cheese

you can use any vegetables that appeal to you

Mix all the ingredients together — shape into patties. Heat some oil in a skillet... brown patties on both sides — place in a baking pan and bake 25 to 30 minutes. Top with a slice of cheddar or jack cheese 5 minutes before done, if desired.

Cyn's Quiche

...very easy & delicious

1 pie shell (see pg. 231)
1 small onion
1 lb. mushrooms
½ lb. cheddar cheese (mild or sharp)
1 cup light cream, Half 'n Half or raw milk
4 well beaten eggs
2 tbsp. butter
¼ tsp. salt
¼ tsp. oregano
¼ tsp. parsley

> It's one of those
> "throw-it-all-together"
> amazing recipes

Make crust. Chop onion and mushrooms and
sauté in butter for 5 minutes ⌣ add salt,
oregano & parsley, Mix and place in pie pan on
top of crust ⌐ place cheese evenly on top of
vegetables. Beat eggs with cream and pour
over vegies and cheese.
Bake at 350° for 45 minutes.

Also good with broccoli instead of mushrooms...
or combination of both. Can use swiss or jack
cheese if you like.

Great for dinner, lunch ⌣ or brunch.

'Wing-It Rice

4 cups cooked brown rice

2 cloves garlic, pressed or chopped
6 scallions, chopped
2 stalks celery, diced
1 carrot, chopped
1 lb. tofu, cubed
½ tsp. fresh grated ginger
½ cup bamboo shoots ⎫
½ cup water chestnuts ⎭ small can (optional) of each
salt & pepper
soya sauce or tamari – and/or Dr. Bronner's (see pg. 233)
4 tbsp. sesame oil (safflower will do, but sesame preferred)

Cook rice early in the day if possible. In a skillet heat 2 tbsp. sesame oil – add 1 clove garlic and half of chopped scallions. Sauté a minute... add remaining vegetables, tofu and ginger. Sauté 10 minutes. Season with salt, a nice sprinkle of pepper and soya sauce. Cover and set aside. In another skillet, heat 2 tbsp. sesame oil – add 1 clove garlic and remaining scallions. Sauté 5 minutes. Add rice – stir well and season with a little tamari. Saute 5 minutes. Mix rice with sautéed vegetables and serve.

Spontaneous Casserole

I made this for an unexpected crowd one evening, using the only ingredients on hand ... it was so good that it has become a favorite, especially with the children!

1 lb. elbow or ziti noodles (artichoke pasta preferred ~ see pg. 236)

1 to 2 cups cottage cheese (use as much or as little as you like)

½ to 1 cup sour cream or plain yogurt

5 tbsp. butter

2 medium zucchini ~ cut in rounds [I leave them big so the kids can pick them out]

2 cakes tofu (1 lb.), cubed in bite-size pieces

4 medium scallions, chopped (or onions)

2 medium cloves garlic, pressed

½ to 1 cup grated sharp Italian cheese (romano, locatella fontina, cheddar or jack will do)

(... I like the Italian cheeses ~ as with zucchini, basil & parsley, the casserole has an Italian flavor to it)

1 tsp. dried parsley

½ tsp. dried basil

herb salt and tamari to taste

Cook pasta as directed. Drain and mix with 3 tbsp. butter. Season with herb salt. Add cottage cheese & sour cream. Mix well. In a skillet, melt 1 tbsp. butter and sauté garlic, onion & zucchini for 5 minutes. Add herbs & tamari. Then add to the noodles. In same skillet you sautéed vegies, melt 1 tbsp. butter and saute tofu till golden on all sides. Sprinkle with tamari. Add to noodles. Then add grated cheese. Mix well. Put into a buttered casserole dish and bake uncovered at 325° for 45 minutes.

Myra's - HOT 'n ZESTY - Stuffed Bread

this is good as an hor d'oeuvre ‿ cut into thin slices ‿ or as a sandwich in larger slices. Also, makes a good camping-out dish!

1 large loaf of french bread
2 onions, sliced thin
2 tomatoes, sliced thin
1 green pepper, chopped } optional
½ lb. mushrooms
½ lb. provolone, jack or mozzarella cheese
oregano
basil
herb salt

Cut loaf in half lengthwise. Scoop out middle of bread. Slice tomatoes, onions, pepper and mushrooms ... and place evenly on sides of bread. Sprinkle with oregano, basil and herb salt, then spread grated cheese evenly on top of vegetables. Close bread and wrap in foil. Bake for 12 minutes in a hot oven.

‿ Slice and serve.

Annie's Soyabean Casserole

~ very tasty !

1½ cups dry soyabeans (cover w/ water & soak overnight.)
  or

Flaked soyabeans are good, too. Cooks
faster. Ask for at health food store

3 cups soaked soyabeans
3 cloves garlic, pressed
2 medium onions, chopped
1 green pepper, chopped
½ lb. mushrooms, chopped
1 medium can tomatoes, crushed
¼ cup tamari
¼ cup oil (for sautéing)
½ tsp. oregano
½ tsp. basil
¼ tsp. thyme
½ lb. grated cheddar or jack cheese (you could
½ cup toasted wheat germ   use more if
paprika   you like)

Cover soaked beans with fresh water and cook, covered,
2 hrs. or till soft (not mushy). Sauté in oil... garlic,
pepper and mushrooms. Add tomatoes, spices & tamari.
Mix with cooked soyabeans and add most of cheese.
Put in casserole dish. Top with wheat germ and remaining cheese and paprika. Bake, uncovered, 45
minutes at 350°.

NOTE: Season well, as soyabeans are bland. Makes a lovely
  golden top.... delicious and great protein.

Zucchini Casserole

· simple & delicious ～ handed from Chuck to Deb

4 zucchini squash
1 lb. sharp cheddar cheese
1 lg. can tomato paste
parsley
oregano
basil
salt & pepper
olive oil

Grate cheese. Wash & slice zucchini. Oil
a 2-qt. casserole with lid. Layer casserole with : a layer of zucchini, sprinkle
of salt & pepper, then a heavier sprinkle of
parsley, oregano & basil. Then add a
layer of cheese and scatter a few dabs of
tomato paste on the top. Sprinkle lightly
with olive oil. Continue to layer until you
reach the top. Cook, covered 1½ to 2 hrs.
at 350°.

Various Pizza Toppings & Stromboli

What's good on a <u>pizza</u>?

    tomato sauce
    mozzarella and/or jack cheese
    parmesan or any other sharp Italian
                      cheeses
    fresh garlic
    onions
    peppers
    mushrooms
    zucchini
    tofu, sliced
    marinated artichoke hearts
    T.V.P. (see pg. 237) ↪ <u>can be added to</u>
    pitted olives   <u>sauce for more</u>
                           <u>umpff</u>!
    oregano, basil, parsley

... sautéing the vegetables in a little olive oil adds a nice flavor.

<u>Stromboli</u> is basically pizza dough, rolled out, with any or all of the above ingredients piled on top ↪ and then the dough is rolled up like a jelly roll. Bake 45 minutes in a hot oven (425°). It's also important to bake pizza in a hot oven.

<u>Candy's Shepherd's Pie</u> ⌐ Vegetarian !

⌐ with or without a pie crust

If using crust,
double pie crust recipe (see pg. 231)

... for using a
9x13 baking pan

6 to 8 medium potatoes
2 cups T.V.P. (see pg. 237)
1 onion, chopped
1 large clove garlic, pressed
1 cup corn kernels
1 cup carrot, diced
1 cup string beans, chopped
1 cup peas

or 1 lb. bag of mixed frozen vegetables

1 to 1½ cups tomato sauce
¼ to ½ lb. grated cheddar cheese (optional)
milk ⌐ about ⅔ cup ⟵ for mashing potatoes
butter or margarine ⌐ about 2 tbsp. ⟵
herb salt
salt & pepper
tamari
paprika

Make crust, if using ⌐ put in a 9 x 13 pan

(... it's great <u>without</u> the crust, too ⌐ and that
                                    much less work !!)

continued ⟶

- In a bowl, soak T.V.P. with 2 cups water and let sit 10 minutes. Wash and cube potatoes ↝ put into a pot and cover with water. Bring to a boil and simmer 15 to 20 minutes or until tender.

- While the potatoes are simmering, melt 2 tbsp. butter in a large skillet and sauté onion & garlic for 5 minutes. Add vegetables and sauté 5 minutes ↝ add tomato sauce. Drain excess water from T.V.P. and add (T.V.P.) to skillet. Season with herb salt and tamari, and let simmer while potatoes are cooking. Drain potatoes and mash, adding salt & pepper, butter and milk to taste.

- Spoon vegie/T.V.P. mixture in bottom of a 9x13" baking pan ↝ sprinkle with half of grated cheese. Carefully spread mashed potatoes over entire top. Sprinkle with remaining cheese and a little paprika.

  Bake at 350° for ½ hour or till potatoes are golden

<u>Tofu Spread</u>

a nice sandwich filling ↝

1 lb. tofu, mashed
½ tsp. garlic powder
¼ tsp. Herbamare
      (see pg. 234)
1 tbsp. Dijon mustard

Mash tofu and add other ingredients.
Mix thoroughly ↝ serve on bread or
bagel with a little cheese, sliced
tomato, sprouts, and a slice of
onion.

↝ Great on crackers, too!

Impromptu Spinach Filo Pie

one night we were invited to an impromtu pot-luck dinner. While rummaging thru my refrigerator, I found the ingredients for what turned out to be a wonderful dish.

Try it — it's _tops_!

- 1 box Filo pastry — sold at cheese stores
- 4 bags spinach (or 4 boxes frozen... I must confess I used frozen that night)
- 1 large onion, diced
- 2 large cloves garlic, pressed
- 1 stick butter
- 1 lb. creamed cottage cheese
- ¼ to ½ lb. feta cheese
- ¼ to ½ lb. cheddar or jack cheese
- a handful of fresh parsley — or 1 tsp. dried
- a nice pinch of oregano
- a nice pinch of basil
- tamari
- herb salt } to taste

Here goes... wash & cook spinach ever so slightly — drain well. Melt 2 tbsp. butter in a pan and sauté onion & garlic about 5 min. Remove from heat and mix with spinach. Then add all other ingredients _except_ filo and remaining butter. Mix well and set aside for a minute. Melt remaining butter — do not scald. Butter a large baking dish (13"x9"x2") and put in about 8 filo leaves. Brush with butter. Put ½ of spinach mixture on _top_. Put 8 more leaves on _top_ of that. Brush w/ butter. Put remaining spinach mixture on _top_. _Top_ with remaining filo and brush w/ remaining butter. Bake at 350° for about 40 min. till _top_ is golden brown & cut into squares. Serve warm.

Classic Macaroni and Cheese

⌐ one of our family favorites... an easy hot dish on a chilly night (or day!)

...we usually have artichoke or whole wheat elbow noodles on hand for this ⌐ but for a nice variety and a new look, try the spirals or the small shells...

8 oz. elbow macaroni
½ lb. sharp cheddar cheese, sliced
½ stick butter or margarine
¼ cup flour

2 cups milk
1¼ tsp. salt
dash of pepper
½ cup grated parmesan

- Cook macaroni 5 minutes (al dente...as the rest of the cooking will take place in the oven), and drain.

- Meanwhile, prepare white sauce: melt butter in medium saucepan ⌐ remove from heat... blend in flour, stir in milk, then seasonings. Bring to a boil, and boil 1 minute, stirring constantly.

- In a buttered casserole or baking dish, alternate macaroni with cheese ⌐ beginning with macaroni on bottom and ending with cheese on top (I lay slices of cheese closely together for each layer...it makes for a heartier, thicker dish.).

- Pour sauce over macaroni and cheese. Sprinkle with parmesan. Bake 20 minutes or until cheese is melted and golden ⌐ in 350° oven.

Jay Bird's Mao Tse Tung or Leftover Rice

"... Ever wonder what to do with that day-old brown rice — cold and lifeless, staring at you from the bottom of that bio-chemical container... here's a simple alternative..."

2 cups day-old rice (you can use fresh!)
1 cup chopped cooked chicken or shrimp (optional)
1 onion, chopped
1 green pepper, chopped
2 cloves garlic
2 large tomatoes, cut into cubes (the secret ingredient!)
2 eggs
1 cup grated cheddar cheese
salt & pepper
tamari

3 tbsp. oil

Heat oil in a large skillet that has a lid — add vegetables (except tomatoes) and chicken or shrimp, if using. Sauté 7 minutes — add rice and season well. Break in eggs... stir a few minutes — add grated cheese. Cover pan and remove from heat. Add tomato cubes — mix and serve.

Italian Spinach Frittata

a nice appetizer for an Italian meal — also good for breakfast, brunch or lunch.

10 eggs
1 lb. chopped fresh raw spinach (wash & drain well)
1 med. onion (slice & then dice)
1 clove garlic, pressed
¼ lb. _freshly_ grated parmesan or other sharp Italian cheese
fresh parsley, chopped (or 1 tsp. dried)
¼ tsp. dried oregano
¼ tsp. dried basil
salt & pepper to taste
2 tbsp. butter
1 tbsp. olive oil

Preheat oven to 350°.
In a skillet, heat oil — sauté onion and garlic 5 minutes... add spinach, parsley, oregano, basil and some salt & pepper — sauté 3 minutes. Beat eggs — season with salt & pepper. Place 2 tbsp. butter into a casserole dish... put in hot oven till butter melts. Remove from oven — swirl to coat bottom. Spoon vegies into casserole — pour eggs on top. Sprinkle with cheese and bake, uncovered, in oven for 10 minutes or till set. Remove from casserole — cut into wedges and serve.

or simply... generously butter a casserole dish

Annie's Famous Chick Pea "Tuna"

This is a picnic favorite that delights _everyone_...
not only vegetarians!

2 cups dry chick peas (Garbonza Beans)
— soak overnight —   ...or else use 2 cans
of cooked chick peas

3 tbsp. mayonnaise
1 stalk celery, diced
1 tsp. dry minced onion
¼ tsp. celery seed
1 tsp. tahini (see pg. 237)
½ tsp. garlic powder
juice of 1 lemon
½ tsp. tamari
1 tsp. paprika
salt & pepper

... just use however you use tuna salad

If you cook your own chick peas, soak overnight —
remove water. Add fresh water to cover and cook
1½ hours or till tender. Drain and mash — leave
chunky. To the mashed chick peas, add the rest of
the ingredients and mix together well.
Chill and serve.

~ Great as filling for sandwiches, especially on a
bagel with sprouts & cheese! Also good as a dip.

the BEST & EASIEST <u>Greek Spinach Pie</u> ever!
~ Spanakipita ~

1 box Filo Dough [delicate pastry leaves] ~ sold in most cheese stores & some super-markets
2 lbs. fresh spinach (or frozen)
1 lb. Feta cheese
2 medium onions, sliced
2 large cloves garlic, crushed (or more if you like... I do!)
½ lb. fresh mushrooms, sliced
juice of 1 lemon
1 stick of butter
lots of fresh parsley (or dried, but fresh is best)
small amount of herb salt (Feta is a salty cheese)
a pinch of basil (optional)

Cook spinach ever so slightly. Drain well & set aside. Melt 5 tbsp. butter in pan — add sliced onion, crushed garlic, sliced mushrooms & parsley. Sauté 5 to 10 min. Add herb salt if desired. Mix spinach with sauteed vegetables. Squeeze the lemon on top (removing seeds). Crumble feta cheese & mix in. Now... take 8 sheets of Filo Dough and place ⅓ spinach mixture about a third of the way from the bottom of sheets (you will be treating this like a jelly roll or strudel) ~ roll up and place on buttered cookie sheet. Repeat with rest of Filo & mixture, making 3 rolls (using approx. 8 sheets at a time & ⅓ spinach mixture for each). You could also do this in a casserole dish, placing 8 sheets on bottom; then ½ spinach; then 8 more sheets; then rest of spinach; and remaining sheets on top. Melt the remaining butter and brush over 'strudels' or casserole. Bake at 350° for about 40 minutes — till golden.

Serve with soup & salad, if serving as an entree... great as a side dish... and as hors d'oeuvres, too.

You can cut the recipe in half, but I prefer to cook in large amounts for freezing and/or leftovers ~ saves time in the end.

serves 6 to 8

Vegetarian Chili

2 cups dried Kidney beans (soaked overnight)
...or 4 cups cooked Kidney beans

2 cups T.V.P. (see pg. 237) — soak in water   4 cups water

2 cups peeled and crushed tomatoes

1 green pepper, chopped

1 large onion, chopped

3 cloves garlic, pressed

2 tbsp. chili powder

1 tbsp. cumin

1 bay leaf

Salt & pepper

Salsa — buy at supermarket or health food store

Cover beans with water and soak overnight. Pour water off in the morning. Place beans in a large heavy pot — add 2 qts. of fresh water & bay leaf. Cover and bring to a boil — reduce heat and simmer for 1 hour. Soak T.V.P. in water for 20 min. Pour off excess water and add to beans. Prepare vegetables & add to pot, along with seasoning. Cover and simmer 1½ to 2 hrs., till beans are tender. Adjust seasoning, adding more chili powder, etc., depending on taste. Serve.

Pass a bowl of salsa around the table. The chili can be served w/ brown rice, if desired.

Onion & Zucchini Quiche

Pie Crust (see pg. 231)

1 small clove garlic, pressed
1 small onion, sliced or diced
2 small chopped zucchini (or 1 med. to large)
½ lb. cheddar cheese, grated
1 cup Half 'n Half or milk
4 eggs, beaten
2 tbsp. butter
½ tsp. marjoram
1 tsp. dried parsley
Salt & pepper to taste
paprika

Make crust as directed. Place in a pie plate.
In a skillet melt butter, and sauté garlic,
onion and zucchini for 5 minutes. Add
herbs and a little salt & pepper. Spoon into
pie plate. In a small bowl beat eggs and
add cream. Sprinkle grated cheese on top
of vegies and pour egg & cream on top.
Sprinkle with paprika and bake 45 minutes
at 350°, or till firm and golden.

Penelope's Broccoli Quiche

Pie Crust (see pg. 231)

1 head broccoli, broken into small flowers
1 large onion, chopped
1 clove garlic, pressed
2 tbsp. butter
fresh parsley, chopped
a pinch of marjoram
2 eggs, beaten
1 cup milk
½ lb. cheddar cheese
herb salt ⎫
tamari   ⎬ to taste
paprika ⎭

Make crust — place in an 8 or 9" pie plate. Melt butter in a skillet — add vegetables, herbs and seasoning... sauté about 7 minutes. Spoon into pie plate on top of crust. Grate or slice cheese & place evenly on top of veggies. Beat eggs & milk together — pour on top of cheese and veggies. Sprinkle with paprika. Bake in a 425° pre-heated oven for 15 minutes. Reduce heat to 350° and bake 30 more minutes.

Serve hot with a salad & soup, or serve at room temperature for a party.

Lo Mein

...a Chinese/Japanese taste treat
with vegetables, tofu and noodles

1 lb. Japanese sobo noodles (see pg. 236) ⏤ sold
at Health Food Stores
or Oriental Markets
2 cakes tofu (1 lb.), cubed
5 or 6 scallions, chopped
2 cloves garlic, pressed
1 stalk celery, sliced
1 head broccoli, cut into bite-size pieces
1 bag sprouted mung beans (sold in most supermarkets)
sesame or safflower oil
tamari to taste
fresh ginger, grated (optional)
sesame seeds (optional)
Dr. Bronner's Liquid Bouillon (optional)
⏤ see pg. 233

In a wok or skillet, sauté garlic, scallions and
tofu about 5 minutes in oil. Add celery, broccoli,
sesame seeds and tamari ⏤ sauté 10 minutes
until vegetables are cooked but still crunchy.
Add sprouts ⏤ cover and remove from fire.

Meanwhile, cook pasta as directed. Drain and
mix with vegetables. Sprinkle with Dr. Bronner's
to adjust seasoning.

serves 6

Tulip Vegetable Pancake

... without the tulips !

Pancake Batter
4 eggs
1 cup flour
1 cup milk
½ tsp. salt
1 tsp. baking powder
1 tbsp. butter

Top with :
1 cup grated jack cheese or any mild cheese

Vegetables
1 small onion, chopped
1 lg. clove garlic, pressed
2 carrots ~ cut in rounds
1 zucchini, in rounds or cubed
½ head broccoli (flowers)
1 stalk celery, sliced
fresh parsley
pinch of thyme & marjoram
pinch of basil
herb salt & pepper
butter

In a bowl mix all batter ingredients. Melt butter in a baking dish and pour in batter. Bake at 450° for 10 minutes. Reduce heat to 350° and bake another 10 minutes or until golden brown. While the pancake is baking, sauté your vegetables till tender but crispy. Season. When pancake is done, spoon vegies on top and sprinkle liberally with cheese. Put under broiler 2 to 5 minutes until cheese melts.

~ A meal in itself...
 Serve with a nice green salad.

Egg Rolls

I used to have to go to an oriental market to buy all my ingredients, but now most supermarkets have it all.

1 pkg. egg roll skins
1 lb. bag mung bean sprouts
1 bunch scallions
1 small head Chinese celery cabbage
1 small can of bamboo shoots ⎱ optional
1 small can of water chestnuts ⎰
2 cakes tofu (1 lb.)
1 clove garlic, pressed
(if you have leftover chicken, chop it up & put it in... 'shrimp' add a nice flavor, too)
tamari or soya sauce
salt & pepper
pinch of ginger
1 lg. bottle (24 oz. size) Peanut Oil for frying

Chop all the vegetables and tofu, and sauté in a skillet with a little oil. Add tamari, ginger, and salt & pepper to taste. Cook 5 to 10 min. Take 1 skin and place a heaping tbsp. of veggies onto it — roll up (a diagram is provided on skin package). Heat the whole bottle of peanut oil in a skillet till very hot (peanut oil is always used by the Chinese, as it will get real hot without burning). Place a few egg rolls in — brown on 1 side, then turn over with tongs, and do the other side. Place on paper towels to drain. Serve with Duck Sauce, which you can buy in the Chinese section of the supermarket; hot mustard is also available.

Denise's Cauliflower & Potato Curry

6 medium potatoes, scrubbed (leave skins on)
1 medium head cauliflower
4 scallions or 1 small onion, chopped
2 large cloves garlic, pressed
2 carrots or zucchini, sliced (optional)
1 tsp. curry powder
½ tsp. cumin
½ tsp. tumeric
¼ tsp. dry mustard
⅛ tsp. coriander }
⅛ tsp. cardamom } optional
herb salt
½ cup water
¼ cup tamari
2 tbsp. butter or oil
1 cup plain yogurt

In a large pan, melt butter... stir in spices and sauté 5 minutes. Add garlic and onions ⌣ sauté 5 more minutes. Wash and cut potatoes into half-inch cubes. Break cauliflower into flowers. Add potatoes and cauliflower to pan. Add other vegetables (if using them), water, herb salt & tamari ⌣ and sauté 10 minutes, stirring often. Add yogurt and heat well. Adjust seasoning.

Serve with brown rice.

Straight from Italy......   authentic
Italian
Manicotti

......this manicotti is
made with a crepe ~
a little extra effort
but well worth it !   [from scratch !]

1 quart spaghetti sauce
                    (see pg. 86)

Manicotti Crepe :

8 eggs
2 cups flour
¾ tsp. salt
oil ~ for cooking crepes

Cheese Filling :

2 lbs. Ricotta cheese
½ lb. mozzarella cheese
                (grated or cubed)
2 tbsp. chopped parsley
¼ lb. grated Italian sharp
                        cheese
to taste { herb salt
         { freshly ground pepper

Prepare or have 1 quart tomato sauce on hand.

To make _filling_ ~ simply combine all the filling ingredients together in a bowl and mix real well ... set aside.

To make _crepes_ ~ in a bowl, beat your eggs & salt ~ add flour a
little at a time, mixing well. Brush a small skillet or crepe
pan with oil ... just enough to coat. Heat well. Then spoon in
about 5 tbsp. of the crepe batter ... rotate pan to spread
batter evenly over entire bottom (if you need a little more
batter, then by all means add another tablespoon ~ you can
make crepes small or large, depending on preference and pan
size). Cook the crepe 1 minute, then flip to other side and
cook 1 more minute. Now ... you have a choice ... you can continue making crepes until all the batter is used up or else you
can stuff each crepe as you finish it. I like to stuff as I go ~
for when you stack the crepes, it is necessary to use waxed
paper between each one to prevent sticking. Cover the bottom
of casserole dish with tomato sauce (approx. 1 cup). Take
a crepe & place about 4 tbsp. of filling in it ~ and roll up like
a jelly roll. Place in casserole dish. When all crepes are
stuffed, spoon remaining sauce on top ~ sprinkle with grated
cheese. Bake at 350° for 30 to 40 min. or till bubbling hot.
                                    ~ _A Winner_ !

Broccoli - Cheese Casserole

~ al la Chuck

a wonderful garlic-y and cheese-y way
to serve broccoli

2 heads of broccoli, cut in flowers (discard
4 lg. cloves garlic,
              pressed

(tough part of
stems)

2 tbsp. butter
½ lb. of muenster cheese (or more), sliced
fresh parmesan cheese (optional)

Prepare broccoli and steam about 5 minutes.
Drain, put back into same pot and cover
(to keep warm) ~ Melt butter in small
pan ~ add garlic and simmer 5 minutes
(careful not to burn). Pour over broccoli
and gently mix together. Put half of broc-
coli-garlic mixture in bottom of a
buttered casserole dish... spread a layer
of sliced cheese on and finish with rest of
broccoli mixture, then cheese, and lastly
with a healthy sprinkle of parmesan cheese
to top it all off. Bake at 350° for 15 to 20
minutes.

Lasagna with Tofu & Spinach

a great lasagna — the tofu absorbs the flavors
of the tomato sauce and adds wonderful protein

1 lb. lasagna noodles
1 qt. spaghetti sauce (see pg. 86)
1 lb. ricotta cheese
½ lb. mozzarella cheese, sliced
2 or 3 cakes of tofu (1 lb.), cubed
1 bag of spinach
¼ lb. grated Italian hard cheese
(parmesan or romano, i.e.)
1 egg, beaten

Cook noodles as directed and drain. Mix ricotta
cheese with egg. Sauté tofu in a little oil, till
golden on all sides. Wash spinach and dry well.
Add to tofu and steam a few minutes. In a
casserole, pour in enough sauce to cover bottom
(sauce should already be seasoned with garlic,
oregano, etc.). Place some lasagna noodles on
top to cover. Spread ⅓ of ricotta mixture on
noodles — then ⅓ tofu/spinach mixture — ⅓
mozzarella — and ⅓ parmesan. Cover with
more noodles and some sauce, and continue
layering. Top with plenty of sauce and bake
uncovered 45 minutes at 350° — till bubbling
hot.
        — GREAT!

Serve with Tracey Righi's Italian Bread — salad
   — wine ... and invite us !!

Zucchini Patties with Parmesan Sauce
or Myra's Wednesday Night's Dinner!

Patties

1½ cups grated zucchini
½ cup grated carrot
1 small finely diced onion
1 garlic clove, pressed
2 tbsp. butter
½ cup milk
1 egg, beaten
8 tbsp. flour (approx.)
a pinch of basil
herb salt & pepper to taste

oil ⌐ for frying

Sauce

½ stick butter
½ cup milk
3 tbsp. flour
1 cup freshly grated Parmesan or Romano cheese

Prepare vegetables & sauté in 2 tbsp. butter for about 8 to 10 min. Set aside. Beat egg and milk together with basil, salt & pepper. Add to cooled vegetables. Add enough flour to allow you to press into a pattie. In a skillet, heat enough oil to barely cover the bottom of the pan ⌐ and fry the patties on both sides till golden. Keep warm in a low oven till sauce is prepared.

To make sauce: melt ½ stick of butter ⌐ add 3 tbsp. flour and stir to make a roux. Add milk and stir well. Heat… but do not bring to a boil…, stirring constantly. Add 1 cup cheese ⌐ simmer a few minutes, stirring constantly. Serve on top of patties.

Harvard Beets

6 to 8 medium beets (allow 1 whole beet per person — depending on how crazy they are about beets)

¼ cup butter

½ cup honey, maple syrup or sugar

½ cup orange juice

1 tbsp. cornstarch

Peel and wash beets. Slice in rounds and add to pot — cover with water and bring to a boil. Reduce heat and cook till tender... about 7 minutes. Drain off liquid. In a small pot, melt ¼ cup butter... add ½ cup honey and ½ cup orange juice. Mix well. Simmer 5 minutes. Stir in cornstarch. Simmer another 3 minutes — pour over beets. Mix and serve.

... peaches, sliced small, and a handful of raisins... are a nice addition at times

Suzy's Stuffed Shells

... just threw this one together at the last minute for some of my Italian relatives ~ and it turned out to be "the best ever tasted"... so they said!

4 dozen large pasta shells
1 onion, diced
1 lb. mushrooms, diced
2 medium zucchini, diced
2 cloves garlic, pressed
1 lb. bag spinach or
    1 box frozen

2 lbs. cottage cheese or ricotta
1 lb. grated mozzarella cheese
½ lb. grated parmesan cheese

1½ quarts tomato sauce
    (see pg. 86)

olive oil

<u>Cook</u> shells until just pliable enough to work with. (Have ready a nicely seasoned Italian-y tomato sauce.)
<u>Saute</u> diced onion, garlic, mushrooms, zucchini in a little olive oil.
<u>Cook</u> spinach slightly and drain well.
<u>Combine</u> cottage cheese (or ricotta) grated mozzarella and parmesan.
<u>Add</u> spinach and sautéed vegetables
<u>Mix</u> all together.

Spoon mixture into shells so they are "stuffed". Cover bottom of pan (13 x 9 Pyrex pan) with a generous amount of sauce and arrange shells snugly to fill pan, filled side up. Cover entirely with sauce and sprinkle some parmesan generously on top.
Bake in moderate oven (325-350°) for 20 minutes or so, till bubbly. Serve.

<u>NOTE:</u> Please keep in mind that all of the above measurements can be varied, depending on your own tastes & how much you want to make. It's nice to have enough for leftovers or for freezing (or both! what a way to stretch a meal ... really worth the little effort it takes!)

Penny's Noodle and Tofu Casserole

1 lb. flat egg noodles
4 cakes tofu (2 lbs.), cubed
1 large head broccoli, cut up
1 medium onion, chopped
mushrooms, if desired, sliced
3 cloves garlic, pressed
2 cups tomato sauce
½ lb. grated cheddar cheese
    (jack cheese is also good)
tamari to taste

Cook noodles as directed. Drain. Put back in pot and add 1 cup tomato sauce. Sauté tofu in a little oil with 1 or 2 cloves garlic till golden. Remove and add to noodles. In same pan, sauté remaining garlic, onions, mushrooms and broccoli. When broccoli is cooked but still crunchy, remove and add to noodles and tofu. Add tamari to taste. Cover bottom of casserole dish with ½ cup tomato sauce. Add noodles, tofu and vegies ↳ and top with grated cheese and remaining sauce.
Bake at 350° for 35 minutes.

a splendid way to prepare...

Acorn or Butternut Squash

acorn or butternut squash (allow ½ squash per person)
butter
honey
a pinch of cinnamon (optional)

Cut squash in half ⁓ remove seeds and into the hollow, place 1 tbsp. butter and 1 tbsp. honey. Place in baking pan (making sure the honey won't spill out).
Bake at 350° for 1 hour ⁓ give or take a little depending on size of squash.
Serve individually.

OR

... you can bake the squashes dry for 1 hr. When finished, scoop out inside and mash. Place in bowl and then add honey and butter.

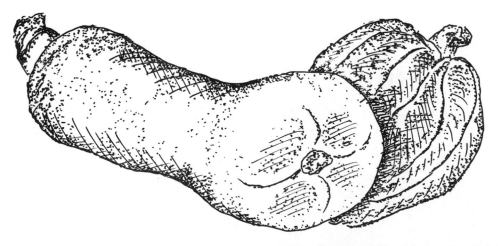

Barley Pilaf

In saucepan, sauté:

  1 large minced onion or 2 slivered leeks
  in ½ stick butter or soy margarine

Add:

  ¾ to 1 lb. fresh sliced mushrooms
  2 stalks celery, sliced and chopped
  ½ cup pine nuts

Stir in:

  1 cup medium barley
  1 tsp. salt, tamari or herb salt
  ½ tsp. thyme
  ½ tsp. marjoram
  ½ rosemary
  ¼ tsp. salt
  ¼ tsp. savory

~ sauté, stirring, to coat barley with butter for 3 minutes.

Add:

  3 cups water or stock (we use vegetable bouillon)

~ bring liquid to boil. Boil 2 minutes. Then put in a casserole dish.

Bake, covered, in preheated 350° oven for 55 minutes.

Stuffed Mushrooms

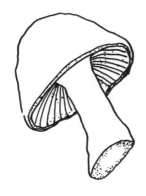

1 lb. large whole fresh mushrooms
3 tbsp. butter
1 onion, chopped
1 large clove garlic, pressed
1 cup bread crumbs (seasoned)
1 cup sour cream
herb salt to taste
½ tsp. parsley
¼ tsp. basil

Melt 1 tbsp. butter in a small pot. Wash mushrooms well and carefully remove stems. Place
mushroom caps on a cookie sheet, top up,
and brush each one with a little melted butter.
Place under broiler 3 min. or so, till lightly
golden. Then set aside. Chop stems with onions
and garlic — and sauté in butter 5 minutes.
Add parsley, basil and herb salt. Mix well.
Add bread crumbs. Mix and add sour cream.
Mix well. Fill the caps with mixture, about
1 tbsp. into each one. Place under broiler 3
to 5 minutes.

⌐ Serve as an hor d'oeuvre or as a vegetable
dish.

Tangy Kale

Kale is a delightful vegetable & very nutritious

1 large bunch of kale, chopped
2 tbsp. oil
1 clove garlic, pressed (optional)
1 tbsp. apple cider vinegar
herb salt

Wash kale real well — shake out excess water and chop. Heat oil and garlic in a skillet and put chopped kale in. Sauté 5 minutes. Then put in about ½ cup water and steam 5 minutes. Drain. Sprinkle on vinegar and herb salt. Mix and serve.

Tofu Spinach Parmesan

2 lbs. tofu (approx. 4 cakes) - allow ½ - ¾ lb. per person
½ lb. mozzarella cheese
1 bag fresh spinach
2 cups spaghetti sauce (see pg. 86)
2 eggs
¾ cup seasoned bread crumbs
olive oil
herb salt to taste

* herbs are cooked into our spaghetti sauce, along with garlic, onions and peppers... mushrooms (if you like)... and a little wine, so do check the sauce recipe before making this dish, for proper seasoning.

Cut the tofu into halves or quarters. Beat egg ... dip tofu into egg, then into bread crumbs - and sauté in olive oil until brown on both sides. Pour about ⅓ of spaghetti sauce into a casserole dish and place breaded tofu on top. Set aside. Wash spinach well and steam ever so slightly. Drain well and place on tofu. Cut the mozzarella cheese into cubes and place on top of each piece of tofu. Cover with the rest of sauce and bake at 350° for 45 minutes or until bubbling.

Serve with fettucini for a real Italian feast... salad, garlic bread and a good red wine!

For eggplant or chicken parmesan - follow the same recipe, substituting eggplant or chicken for tofu. If the idea of spinach doesn't send you, just omit it.

Broccoli Sesame

ᕲan interesting way to enhance broccoli

    1 large head of broccoli
    2 tbsp. sesame seeds
    2 tbsp. butter
    tamari or herb salt

Wash broccoli and cut into flowers. Steam for 10 minutes or less. Do _not_ overcook! Drain. In a skillet, toast sesame seeds till they smell nutty. Add butter and melt. Add tamari or herb salt to taste. Pour over broccoli. Toss lightly & serve.

Vegetable Curry

1 medium broccoli, cut into flowers
1 medium onion, sliced
2 medium garlic cloves, pressed
2 carrots, chopped
1 stalk celery, chopped
1 small can of crushed tomatoes
1 tsp. curry powder (mild or hot)
½ tsp. cumin
½ tsp. tumeric
tamari to taste (or soya sauce)
1 cup plain yogurt
2 cups cooked brown rice

Sauté onion & garlic in a little oil (safflower is good) ⌣ about 5 minutes. Add celery, carrots and broccoli. Sauté another 5 minutes or so. Add tomatoes, spices & tamari. Cover and cook till broccoli and carrots are tender (don't overcook ⌣ the vegies taste great a little crunchy... and the less cooked, the better for you!). Add yogurt right before serving. Spoon over rice and serve with Indian Cucumber Raita (see pg. 26).

(if you like it spicier ⌣ add <u>more</u> curry powder)

Broiled Tomatoes w/ Cheese

when tomatoes are abundant ~ try
this for a change... good side-dish
for fish or chicken.

Slice tomatoes in rounds ~ sprinkle
with salt & pepper, and freshly
grated parmesan or romano cheese
and a pinch of oregano. Place under
broiler for 5 minutes ~ serve.

Delectable Corn Custard
(or Pudding)

this can be used either for a mouth watering
vegetable served along with your main dish,
or for a dessert vegetable - delectable!

4 cups fresh corn (or 1½ lbs. frozen corn)
4 large eggs
1 pint Half 'n Half
¼ cup honey
½ tsp. salt
¼ cup melted butter

Cook corn ever so slightly and let cool. Beat
eggs and add Half 'n Half, honey, salt
and melted butter. Add to the cooled corn.
Pour into a buttered 9 x 9" square cake
pan. Set cake pan into another larger
pan. Pour into larger pan enough hot
water to come ¼ way up the sides of the
custard pan.
Bake at 400° for approximately 35 to 45
minutes ⌐ until _firm_ and golden brown.

Scalloped Potatoes

8 medium potatoes ~ sliced thin (I usually use the slit side of a 4-sided grater.)
1 small onion, sliced thin (optional)
½ stick butter or margarine
2 cups milk
¼ lb. grated cheddar cheese
salt & pepper to taste
paprika
1 tsp. dried parsley (optional)

Butter a 9 x 13" baking dish. Cut or grate potatoes ~ put into dish... top with onion and cheese. In a pot, melt butter ~ add milk, salt & pepper and parsley. Pour over potatoes ~ sprinkle with paprika. Bake in 350° oven for 1 hour or till golden brown, and potatoes are tender when pierced with a fork.

↪ goes well with practically anything !

<u>Bo's Blooming Brussel Sprouts</u>

. . . let's face it ∽ brussel sprouts can use all the help they can get !!

1 pint brussel sprouts
2 tbsp. Dijon mustard
½ cup light cream or Half 'n Half

Wash brussel sprouts and steam for 10-15 minutes. Drain. While the sprouts are steaming, pour ½ cup of cream into small pot and add mustard. Stir till thickens ∽ about 3 minutes. Pour over brussel sprouts. Mix well and serve.

Fabulous Fettucini

⌐ do not eat if dieting because it's too
hard to resist... take it from us !!

1 lb. fettucini noodles
½ lb. sharp Italian cheese (fontinella, romano, locatella or parmesan)
4 tbsp. butter or margarine
1 cup light cream or Half 'n Half
1 or 2 large cloves garlic, pressed
1 tsp. fresh or dried parsley, chopped
freshly ground pepper
salt

Grate cheese (only fresh will do — do not use cheese from jar). Set aside. Cook noodles as directed and drain — return to pot. While the noodles are cooking, melt butter in a saucepan (don't burn) ⌐ add garlic and parsley and simmer 5 minutes. Add cream and simmer 5 minutes longer. Pour over noodles and add cheese. Toss well & serve immediately. Pass around a pepper mill.

NOTE: TIMING IS OF THE ESSENCE WHEN SERVING FETTUCINI... IT MUST BE SERVED IMMEDIATELY ⌐ WHILE IT'S HOT!

serves 4

Glazed Carrots

3 or 4 carrots
· water to steam ·
¼ cup honey
2 tbsp. butter
juice of 1 orange
1 tsp. arrowroot flour or
      corn starch

Clean and cut carrots in rounds.
Steam till tender... about 10 min.
In a small pot, melt butter ⌐
add honey and orange juice.
Mix in arrowroot and stir till it
thickens slightly. Remove from
heat and pour over carrots.
Mix well and serve immediately.

x

Festive Candied Sweet Potatoes

~ a wonderful Holiday dish!

Yams or sweet potatoes (1 per person ... about 8 for this recipe)
¼ cup butter or margarine
¾ cup honey or maple syrup
1 tsp. grated orange rind
1 cup dried apricots
½ tsp. cinnamon (optional)
½ cup chopped walnuts

NOTE: sometimes I add a small can of crushed pineapple (unsweetened) to honey and butter mixture ... a handful of raisins is a nice treat, also

Put potatoes in pot ~ cover with water. Boil until potatoes are half soft ... drain and cool. Remove skins. Cut potatoes in quarters and place in buttered casserole dish.

In saucepan, melt ¼ cup butter ~ add ¾ cup honey and 1 tsp. grated orange rind.

Soak 1 cup dried apricots in 1 cup water ~ till they swell a little. Drain. Add to butter & honey. Add ½ tsp. cinnamon. Mix. Pour over potatoes and bake 45 minutes. Add ½ cup chopped walnuts and bake 10 minutes or so longer.

Parsley Potatoes

8 medium red bliss potatoes
water
1 clove garlic, pressed
2 tbsp. butter
2 tbsp. freshly chopped parsley
       (or 1 tbsp. dried)
herb salt & pepper to taste

Wash and peel potatoes — place in a pot.
Cover with water and bring to a boil.
Reduce heat and simmer 20 minutes
or till potatoes are tender, but not
mushy. Drain — put cover back on and
set aside.
In a small pot, melt butter — add
garlic, parsley and salt & pepper. Simmer
5 minutes ... then pour over potatoes
and serve.

Brussel Sprouts

⌣ lemon & nutmeg

... here's something delicious you can do with brussel sprouts!

1 pint brussel sprouts
1 tbsp. butter
½ lemon
½ tsp. nutmeg

Wash and steam brussel sprouts about 10 minutes. Drain.

To make sauce: melt butter, squeeze lemon into butter and add nutmeg. Stir. Pour over brussel sprouts and serve.

... butter, lemon and nutmeg are wonderful on steamed broccoli and cauliflower as well.

Myra's "TUESDAY · NIGHT'S · DINNER"

~ a simple crustless quiche ~

6 eggs, beaten
1 cup grated cheddar or jack cheese
1 cup milk
¾ cup flour
4 tbsp. butter

Season with : ½ tsp. herb salt
              ¼ tsp. dried parsley
              pinch of marjoram

You can sauté any vegetables and add to this ~ some good ones are :

garlic	broccoli
onion	peppers
zucchini	mushrooms

Melt butter ~ add flour to make a roux... slowly add eggs, milk and spices, stirring constantly. Then add cheese. Pour into a buttered baking pan and bake 30 minutes or till firm and golden.

~ Serve with a hearty soup and
            a loaf of bread !

Seafood Entrées

Carolina's Jumbo Crab Cakes

enough for 4 to 6 adults, and a few for the freezer...
also nice for lunch/sandwich variation

◈ Have ready :
   2 lbs. fresh lump crab meat (or 2 1-lb. cans)

◈ Remove any shells. Put in large bowl and add
the following ingredients :

   ½ cup chopped parsley
   2 tbsp. Worcestershire Sauce
   1 tsp. paprika
   ¼ to ½ tsp. cayenne pepper (how _hot_ do you like them ?!)
   1 tsp. dry mustard
   3 to 4 drops Tabasco
   3 slightly beaten eggs
   2 tsp. horseradish
   1 tbsp. fresh chopped dill } optional
   1 tbsp. mayonnaise
   3 tbsp. minced scallions
   1 tbsp. chopped celery (optional)
   a pinch each of mace, cloves & ginger
   salt & pepper to taste
   oil for frying

Mix thoroughly. Chill. Make into large patties.
Dredge lightly in fresh bread crumbs and
fry till golden.

Scallop & Shrimp Provencale

2 lbs. scallops and 1 lb. shrimp
½ cup white or red wine (sherry is nice, too)
juice of 1 lemon
4 fresh tomatoes, peeled (you may use a small can of peeled tomatoes)
2 medium cloves garlic, pressed
2 tbsp. butter
½ tsp. basil
½ tsp. parsley
herb salt & pepper to taste

In a skillet, melt butter ～ and add garlic.
Sauté 3 minutes or so. Add scallops,
shrimp and other ingredients ～ and
simmer about 7 to 10 minutes.
Serve over rice.

～ Garnish with fresh parsley sprigs or
watercress.

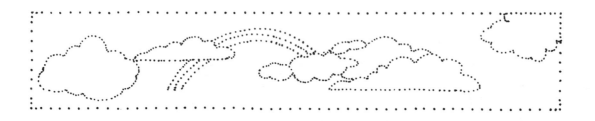

Sweet and Sour Shrimp

~ Tempura ~

You can make this scrumptious meal with chicken, too... or with vegetables, using a different sauce - if you wish - or the same! You can even make tofu tempura!

1½ to 2 lbs. uncooked shrimp
2 eggs beaten
juice of 1 lemon
¼ cup sherry (if you prefer to leave out sherry, just use ¼ c. water)
dash of tamari
dash of herb salt
1 cup flour
1 clove garlic, pressed
a pinch of ginger   } optional
a pinch of coriander
oil (peanut oil preferred ~ see pg. 235)

Sauce:

1 16-oz. can cubed or crushed pineapple, with juice

½ cup ketchup or tomato sauce
a little ginger
1 clove garlic, pressed (optional)
dash of tamari
1 tbsp. cornstarch

continued →

<u>Make sauce first</u> — put all ingredients, except cornstarch, in a saucepan. Bring to a low boil — then add cornstarch and lower flame. Stir constantly for about 5 minutes, till it thickens slightly. Set aside.

<u>Now</u> . . . for the shrimps! Wash and peel, and set aside. In a large bowl, beat eggs . . . squeeze in lemon (don't forget to remove the seeds) — add a little flour — then sherry — and more flour, till it is a smooth batter (like a pancake batter). Add parsley, basil, a pinch of herb salt and tamari. In a wok or skillet, put in about ½ inch of peanut oil. Let oil get <u>very</u> hot . . . you can test by dropping a little water into it — if it really sizzles, it's hot! Add shrimp to batter all at once & mix well till completely coated. Then pour the whole mixture into the hot oil (like one over-sized pancake!). Cook about 5 min. on one side, then flip the whole thing over and cook other side 5 min. Remove from heat and put on paper towel to drain for a minute. Place on platter — pour sauce on top & serve. — Good with 'Wing It Rice (see pg. 108)

Seafood Bisque

1 lb. chopped white fish fillets (haddock, cod, halibut)
½ lb. chopped shrimp, shelled
½ lb. scallops
2 quarts water
1 carrot, chopped
1 onion, chopped
1 clove garlic, pressed
½ cup sherry
2 cups light cream
1 stick butter
5 tbsp. flour

fresh parsley, chopped
a pinch of thyme
a pinch of marjoram
a pinch of tarragon
salt & pepper to taste
1 bay leaf (optional)
paprika

In a heavy 4 quart soup pot place all vegetables and the water ~ bring to a boil, reduce heat and simmer ½ hour. Add all fish ~ simmer 10 minutes. With slotted spoon, remove all the large pieces of vegetables and fish ~ blend in a blender or food processor. Return to pot. In a small saucepan, melt butter ~ add flour and stir to make a smooth roux. Add cream and sherry ~ stir well. Add to soup pot. Add herbs and seasoning to pot... stir and simmer 10 minutes or so, but do not boil. Sprinkle each individual serving with paprika.

<u>Shrimp Scampi</u>

Delicious yet takes very little time to prepare

2 lbs. raw medium to large shrimp
3 cloves garlic, pressed
juice of 1 lemon
½ stick butter
1 tsp. dried parsley
¼ cup sherry
salt & pepper to taste

Shell shrimp — place in baking pan. In a small pot, melt butter — add remaining ingredients and simmer 5 minutes. Pour over shrimp and broil 5 minutes until shrimp are cooked... do not overcook.

Serve over rice.

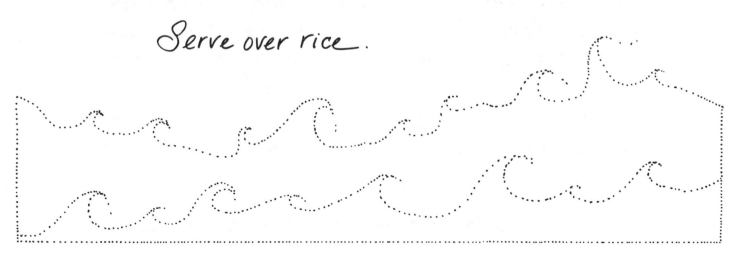

Seafood and Vegetable Frittata

...an exquisite, light yet satisfying summer dinner

½ lb. raw shrimp ⎫ ·or you could use all of one
½ lb. scallops ⎬ or the other if you prefer
1 clove garlic, pressed
3 scallions, chopped
1 medium zucchini, diced
1 cup fresh corn Kernals
a few sprigs of fresh parsley or 1 tsp. dried
10 eggs
½ to 1 cup grated cheddar or jack cheese
3 tbsp. butter
salt & pepper to taste

Remove shells from shrimp. Prepare vegetables, and in a large skillet, melt 3 tbsp. butter and add vegetables. Sauté 5 minutes. Add shrimp and scallops. Cover and cook 8 minutes. Beat eggs. Add salt & pepper and pour over vegetables and shrimp. Cook on low heat till eggs set but are still moist on top. Sprinkle with cheese. Cover and remove from heat. Allow frittata to sit for a few minutes to allow cheese to melt.

Serve with a large salad & a hearty bread!

Black Peppered Shrimp

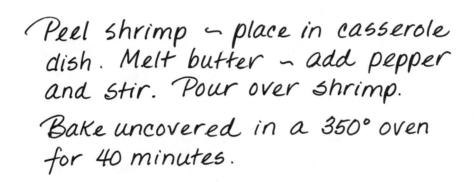

2 lb. large uncooked shrimp
2 sticks butter
1 tbsp. freshly ground
                    black pepper

Peel shrimp ~ place in casserole
dish. Melt butter ~ add pepper
and stir. Pour over shrimp.
Bake uncovered in a 350° oven
for 40 minutes.

... then gather 'round with
warmed french bread for
unbelievably delicious dipping !!

Al and Mieko's Barbecued Squid

People usually cringe at the mention of squid !!!
But once they try this, they love it !

Squid ～ allow ½ lb. per person
   (if you can't get the squid sliced & skinned
     already... just forget the whole thing !!)

soya sauce or tamari

garlic, crushed

juice of 1 lemon

Mix soya sauce, garlic and lemon together.
Place squid in a bowl ～ pour marinade
over and refrigerate a few hours.
Barbecue squid on charcoal, about 5
minutes on each side.

"I'm a squiddy·did kid
and if you don't do as
I bid, I'll bite you !"
   ～ as sung by Peter's
       dog, Champy !

Fish Casserole

This is an unusual way to prepare fish
... simple, but quite delicious.

3 lb. Haddock fillets or any mild white fish
½ stick butter
juice of 1 lemon
tamari
1 large clove garlic, pressed
2 stalks celery, chopped
2 scallions, chopped
6 to 8 oz. crabmeat, fresh or canned
½ cup bread crumbs
½ to ¾ cup Half 'n Half
½ tsp. tarragon
½ tsp. dried parsley
paprika
black pepper

In a buttered casserole dish that has a cover, line bottom with enough fish fillet to cover. Sprinkle with a little tamari and squeeze some lemon on top. Put a couple pats of butter on top, then repeat the same layering till all fish is used. Then, melt 2 tbsp. butter in skillet and sauté garlic, scallions and celery for 5 minutes. Add crabmeat, bread crumbs, tarragon, parsley and pepper ↝ mix well. Place crabmeat mixture on top of fish. Sprinkle with paprika and pour Half 'n Half on top. Bake at 350° for ½ hour.

↝ Serve with corn-on-the-cob and a green salad.

Russian Salmon

I served this to some friends one night and they loved it. When I told them how I made it, they were surprised that something so good could be so simple to prepare. Donald said that when he was a kid and his mom said they were having salmon for dinner, his face would turn white! But he loved this one.

Sauce — Russian Dressing
(see pg. 50)

Salmon steaks or fillets
(allow ½ lb. per person)

lemon

Simply make your Russian Dressing. Place salmon (if fillet, skin side down) in a broiling pan. Squeeze lemon over fish. Spread your Russian Dressing on top and broil 10 to 15 minutes, or till fish flakes when tried with fork.

Serve with a salad, parsley potatoes (see pg. 142), and a steamed vegetable.

Summer Dill Fillets

2 lbs. of flounder, lemon sole or any other mild white fish
juice of 1 lemon
1 cup sour cream
1 tsp. dill
1 small clove garlic, pressed
2 scallions, chopped
¼ lb. fresh sliced mushrooms ⌐ optional
paprika

Wash fish and place on a baking pan. Squeeze lemon over. Mix sour cream with garlic, dill and scallions (and mushrooms, if desired). Spread evenly over fish fillets. Sprinkle with paprika.
Bake at 450° for 10 minutes... then place under broiler for 5 minutes.

Serve with salad, parsley potatoes (see pg. 151) and broccoli sesame (see pg. 142)

Simple & Delicious Breaded Haddock

- 1½ lbs. Haddock fillets (flounder, or any mild white fish will do)
- ½ cup seasoned or plain bread crumbs
- juice of 1 lemon
- 2 tbsp. tamari (or soya sauce)
- butter

. . . .

Wash and dry haddock. Place on platter; squeeze lemon over it and sprinkle tamari over all. Then take bread crumbs and place in a plastic bag (watch out for holes!) Take one filet... put in bag and shake till evenly coated. Repeat with remaining fish. Place in a buttered baking dish and dab a little butter on top, if you wish. Bake at 350° for one-half hour or so... till flaky when touched with fork. Serve with tartar sauce (if desired), buttered noodles, broccoli and salad. Quite a slimming meal!

. . . . . then you won't feel so bad when you have STRAWBERRY~CHOCOLATE PIE for dessert! (see pg. 220)

NOTE: I have found that haddock gets chewy if overcooked. Fish should be _just_ cooked thru.

<u>Oriental Scallop and Vegetable Sauté</u>
↳ over rice

1 lb. scallops (bay or sea)
1 red or green bell pepper, sliced
4 scallions, chopped
1 large clove garlic, pressed
a little freshly grated ginger (optional)
1 medium zucchini, chopped
1 stalk celery, chopped
a few sprigs fresh parsley or ½ tsp. dried.
½ cup pine nuts (optional)
½ cup sliced water chestnuts (optional)
3 tbsp. butter
Salt & pepper to taste
3 tbsp. tamari or soya sauce
2 tbsp. lemon juice
3 tbsp. sherry (optional)
2 tbsp. prepared Dijon mustard

Cook 1½ cups raw rice as directed.
Prepare vegetables. In a skillet melt butter, and
sauté vegetables 5 minutes. Add scallops &
all other ingredients ↳ and sauté 10 minutes.

Serve over rice.

<u>Spaghetti with White Clam Sauce</u>

1 lb. spaghetti noodles (I use artichoke noodles ~
                                          see pg. 236)

1 quart fresh shelled clams (juice and all)
3 large cloves garlic, pressed
4 tbsp. butter
fresh parsley or 1 tsp. dried
¼ tsp. oregano
¼ tsp. basil
¼ cup dry white wine (optional)
salt & pepper to taste
½ lb. freshly grated romano or parmesan
                                       cheese

Grate cheese ~ set aside.
Begin cooking pasta. Meanwhile, in a medium
pot melt butter ~ add garlic and simmer 5
minutes. Add remaining sauce ingredients, and
simmer 10 to 15 minutes or till pasta is finished.
Drain pasta well and pour clam sauce over it.
Mix well. Serve immediately.

   ~ pass the grated cheese around the table.

Selma's Filet of Flounder Florentine

2 lbs. flounder fillets (sole or any mild fish can be used)

1 lb. fresh spinach (1 pkg. frozen if you prefer)

1 cup sour cream

½ cup chopped scallions

1 lemon

½ cup grated cheddar or mild cheese

½ cup bread crumbs or wheat germ (or ¼ cup of each)

1 tsp. sesame seeds (optional)

Butter a casserole dish. Place ½ of fish on bottom and squeeze ½ lemon over same. Cook spinach slightly and drain well. Mix sour cream and scallions with spinach, and spoon over fish. Place remaining fish on spinach and squeeze ½ lemon on top. Sprinkle with bread crumbs, sesame seeds, and grated cheese.
Bake at 350° for ½ hour.

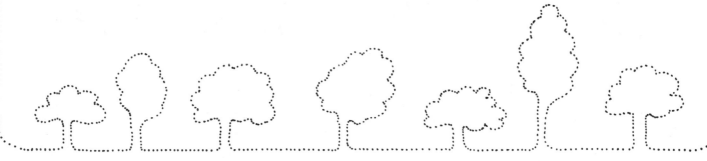

Debby's Fish Casserole
↳ great cooked in a clay casserole

1½ lbs. white fish fillets (flounder, sole or haddock)
8 oz. shredded cheddar cheese
1 cup bread crumbs
8 oz. fresh sliced mushrooms
butter
salt & pepper to taste
1 to 1½ cups white wine
fresh parsley

Mix cheese and bread crumbs together. Layer the casserole with fish ↳ place sliced mushrooms on top along with freshly chopped parsley. Generously sprinkle with bread crumbs and cheese. Dot with butter. Pour 1½ cups wine over all.

Bake in covered clay pot ½ hour at 425.° or Bake in regular covered casserole 40 min. at 350°

Japanese Hoisin Salmon

~an unusual & luscious way to transform salmon! Hoisin sauce is an oriental dark bean paste... a kind of a dark barbecue sauce (can be found at most supermarkets and oriental markets).

2 lbs. fresh salmon steaks or fillets
juice of 1 lemon
1 clove garlic, pressed
1 cup Hoisin sauce
2 scallions, chopped (for garnish)

Place salmon on a broiling pan and squeeze lemon on top. Add garlic to Hoisin sauce & spread evenly over salmon. Broil 10 to 15 min. (check with fork to see when fish is cooked~ it should be flaky). Place on serving dish. Garnish with chopped scallions and serve with rice and a steamed vegetable.

Poached Lemon Sole with Broccoli

2 lb. lemon sole fillets (flounder, scrod, or any mild fish will do)
1 bunch broccoli
3 tbsp. butter
½ cup white wine
¼ cup thinly sliced onion or scallions
1 bay leaf
2 tbsp. lemon juice
¼ tsp. tarragon

Cut broccoli into flowers (try to cut into as many pieces as you have fillets). Steam about five minutes or so. Remove from water. Wrap a fish fillet around each flower. Combine remaining ingredients in small saucepan and heat. Put fish and broccoli in a casserole dish and pour warmed butter mixture over. Cover and bake 10 minutes or until fish is flaky. Place on serving dish and spoon liquid over fish.

Serve with rice.

Chicken Entrées

Chicken Paprika

1 chicken, cut up in parts
1 onion, diced
2 cloves garlic
1 cup sour cream
1 cup chicken broth
2 tbsp. paprika
salt & pepper to taste
2 tbsp. butter
parsley ~ 1 tsp. dried

Wash chicken. In a large skillet, melt butter ~ add onion and garlic, and sauté 5 minutes... or till onion is transparent. Add chicken and brown for 10 minutes. Add broth and paprika ~ stir well. Cover and simmer 25 min. Add sour cream, parsley and salt & pepper. Mix well. Heat but do not bring to a boil.
Serve over rice or buttered noodles.

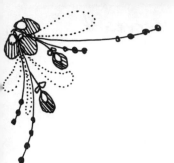

Mimi's Best Chicken

3 to 4 boneless, skinless <u>whole</u> chicken breasts
1 cup Italian dressing (see pg. 45)
1 pkg. dry onion soup mix (Hain has a
                            natural one - check
                            health food stores)

1 medium can of crushed tomatoes or use
                            fresh peeled

½ lb. fresh mushrooms, sliced
3 bay leaves
½ tsp. basil
½ tsp. oregano

... this is one of those
deliciously simple dishes that
fills the whole house with an
irresistable aroma !

Place washed chicken breasts in a 9x 13" Pyrex
pan. Slice mushrooms and place on top of
chicken, along with tomatoes and bay leaves.
Make Italian dressing and mix with onion
soup mix ~ pour over chicken ... sprinkle with
basil and oregano.
Bake uncovered 1 hour at 350°, basting
                            frequently.

Serve with rice ~ or try Mimi's special
touch of fettucini on the side ... now,
that's a meal to remember !

The Bergermeister's Sweet & Sour Chicken

...Delightful!

4 to 6 semi-boneless chicken breasts
2 cups <u>whole</u> cranberry sauce (see bottom of page
               to make your own, or you could use canned)
1 cup orange juice
1 tbsp. vinegar
¼ cup soya sauce
¼ cup sherry (optional)
2 large cloves garlic, pressed
a little freshly grated ginger (optional)
3 tbsp. salt
2 tbsp. oil
3 tsp. cornstarch or arrowroot (see pg. 233)
4 scallions, chopped
1 green pepper, sliced
½ lb. mushrooms, sliced
a small can of drained bamboo shoots }
a small can of water chestnuts } optional
snowpeas can also be added a few minutes
before ready to serve

Wash & dry chicken – press garlic and mix with salt – rub onto chicken. Heat oil in a large skillet and brown chicken slightly. Mix cranberry sauce, orange juice, soya sauce, sherry & vinegar together. Pour over chicken. Cover & simmer 30 min. Remove about a ½ cup of liquid from skillet. Place in a cup – add cornstarch or arrowroot. Mix well. Pour back into skillet – stir – add scallions, peppers & other vegies. Cover & simmer about 7 min. Serve over rice. Garnish with orange slices.

<u>To make cranberry sauce</u>: simply place a 1 lb. bag fresh cranberries & 1 c. water into a pot. Bring to boil. Add ½ c. honey & simmer 10 min.

serves 4

<u>Orange Chicken</u> !

... with orange marmalade
and soya sauce

1 chicken, cut up (or 4 whole breasts)
juice of 1 lemon
1 cup orange marmalade
½ cup soya sauce or tamari

Wash chicken — place in oiled casserole
dish ... squeeze lemon over it. Mix
marmalade with soya sauce and spoon
over chicken, turning to coat well.
Cover and bake 45 minutes. Remove
cover and bake 10 minutes longer.

↳ Serve with parsley potatoes (see pg. 151)
and a steamed vegetable.

Brunswick Stew with Dumplings

ᴖ a hearty meal for a cold blustery day !

> ... it may look complex but it's really very simple
> to make. Don't let the long list of ingredients
> throw you... it doesn't take long to prepare.

1 chicken, cut up
2 quarts water
2 cups crushed & peeled tomatoes
2 cloves garlic, pressed
1 onion, chopped
1 carrot, chopped
1 stalk celery, chopped
a nice amount of fresh parsley (or 1 tsp. dried)
6 potatoes (red bliss are good ᴖ skins & all)
1 cup lima beans, fresh or frozen
1 cup corn, fresh or frozen
herb salt
salt & pepper to taste
¼ tsp. sage   ⎫
¼ tsp. rosemary ⎬ or 1 tsp. poultry seasoning
¼ tsp. thyme   ⎭
4 tbsp. flour ᴖ to thicken

Dumplings: 6 eggs
1 stick softened butter
1 tbsp. dried parsley
1½ cups flour
½ tsp. salt

continued ⋯⟶

In a covered soup pot place your washed chicken and cover with 2 quarts of water. Cover and bring to boil ∽ reduce heat & simmer 1 hour. Remove chicken from pot. Leave broth in pot. Set chicken aside to cool. Wash and chop vegetables ∽ put into broth and simmer ½ hour. Add tomatoes. Remove chicken from bones and add to pot. Simmer 10 minutes. Spoon out a cup of liquid and mix in 4 tbsp. flour to form a thick paste. Pour back into stew ∽ season well and stir.

Make dumplings ∽

reminder...
6 eggs
1 stick soft butter
1 tbsp. dried parsley
1½ cups flour
½ tsp. salt

Beat eggs, add softened butter ∽ and salt & parsley. Mix well. Add flour and blend. Drop by tablespoonfuls into stew. Simmer 20 minutes.

Serve with a crusty bread ... salad ...
and a fine wine.

Nanny Ethel's Chicken

... a quick, yet very tasty way to prepare chicken.

Chicken (allow 1 breast per person)
1 orange (I like to use 1 lemon, too)
wine
tamari or soya sauce
dried parsley
dried basil
paprika
black pepper
poultry seasoning

Wash chicken and place on a broiling pan. Squeeze lemon and orange on top. Sprinkle liberally with tamari and a little wine. Sprinkle with parsley, basil, poultry seasoning, pepper and lots of paprika. Bake 45 minutes, basting every 10 minutes.

Serve with salad, broccoli sesame (see pg. 142) — for a light and satisfying meal... or add macaroni and cheese (see pg. 122) for heartier fare.

Sheryl's DYNAMITE 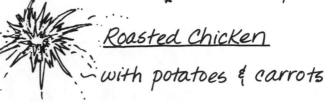 Roasted Chicken

~ with potatoes & carrots

I knew this chicken was going to be great ~ just by the smell, even before it went in the oven... ♡... it's unique ~ try it.

7 lb. roasting chicken	tamari
	garlic powder
8 potatoes	herb salt
8 carrots	parsley
3 onions	chives
1 clove garlic	poultry seasoning
	(thyme, sage, marjoram, rosemary)
	salt & pepper
	paprika
	basil
	Dr. Bronner's Liquid
	(optional) Bouillon
	(see pg. 233)

a lot of all of these !

NOTE: it is impossible to give exact measurements for this creation but I'll tell you just what Sheryl told me to do.

Wash your chicken and remove giblets. Sprinkle evenly over chicken: tamari & Dr. Bronner's, along with herb salt, parsley, chives, poultry seasoning, paprika, basil, garlic powder, salt & pepper. Put a garlic clove and an onion in the cavity and place in a roasting pan (with lid). Wash potatoes (allow 1 per person), cut carrots into large chunks, cut up 2 onions in quarters and place vegetables around chicken in pan. Cover and roast 2 hours, basting chicken and vegetables frequently. Uncover to brown ½ hour longer.

This is also a good way to prepare turkey and you could stuff it if you like, too ~ with Rice Stuffing (see pg. 100)

Teriyaki Chicken .... OR

the secret to making good teriyaki chicken is not only the marinade, but also how long you let it marinate. Overnight is best, but several hours is a must! That way the chicken will be flavorful throughout... not just on the surface.

Shrimp, Swordfish or Tofu

Marinade — for 1 to 2 chickens

½ cup tamari
½ cup Dr. Bronner's Liquid Bouillon (see pg. 233)
  (or if not available, use 1 cup tamari)
juice of 1 lemon
2 cloves garlic, pressed
½ cup sherry
½ tsp. grated ginger (fresh preferred)
2 tbsp. Dijon mustard — optional

Mix all the above ingredients. Wash and dry chicken. Put in a container or bowl. Pour marinade over chicken. Mix to coat well. Refrigerate. Turn chicken every few hours or so.

Authentic teriyaki is always charcoal broiled. Baste while cooking. If you cannot broil over charcoal, broil in the oven.

Curried Chicken

﹀ A WINNER! Impressive, but really very easy
to put together. Inexpensive... great for a crowd.

1 whole chicken, cut up (if you prefer, you could use 4 whole breasts)
water
2 large cloves garlic, crushed
1 onion, diced
2 zucchini, cut large or small
handful of parsley — 1 tbsp., if using dried
2 tbsp. butter (for sautéing)
2 to 3 tsp. curry powder (depending on how hot you like it)
salt to taste
½ tsp. cumin
½ tsp. tumeric } add more if you like
1½ cups sour cream or plain yogurt
½ to 1 cup raisins (optional - try them... great!)
2 cups cooked brown rice (packaged rice pilaf can be used if you prefer)

Wash chicken — put in soup pot and cover with water. Bring to boil — reduce heat and simmer for 45 min. Remove chicken to bowl to cool and _save_ broth. Meanwhile, in skillet melt about 2 tbsp. butter. Add crushed garlic, onion, zucchini and parsley. Sauté till onion is transparent... about 5 min. or so. Remove all chicken from bones and cut into bite-size pieces. Add to garlic & onions. Cover with broth (about 2 cups). Add spices & raisins. Cover and simmer 20 min. Add sour cream right before serving. Spoon over rice and dig in!

Chicken Marsala

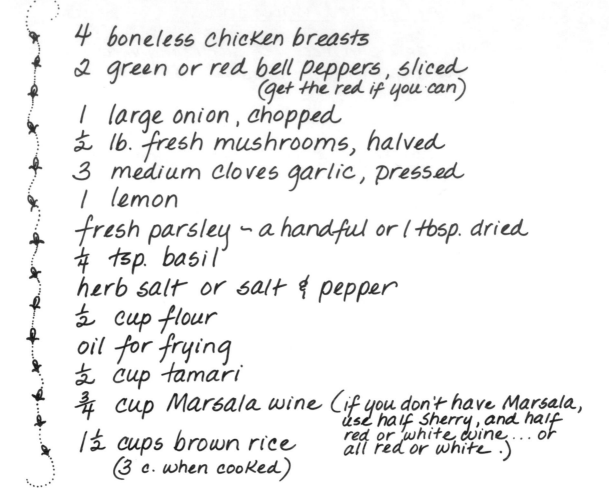

4 boneless chicken breasts

2 green or red bell peppers, sliced
(get the red if you can)

1 large onion, chopped

½ lb. fresh mushrooms, halved

3 medium cloves garlic, pressed

1 lemon

fresh parsley ~ a handful or 1 tbsp. dried

¼ tsp. basil

herb salt or salt & pepper

½ cup flour

oil for frying

½ cup tamari

¾ cup Marsala wine (if you don't have Marsala, use half Sherry, and half red or white wine ... or all red or white.)

1½ cups brown rice
(3 c. when cooked)

Cook rice as directed. Wash chicken and cut each breast into bite-size or larger pieces (I prefer the larger size, as it's less work for me & people can cut up their own ... it's deliciously tender!) Squeeze lemon over chicken. Place flour and herb salt (or salt & pepper) into a plastic bag ~ put a few pieces of chicken in and shake to coat. Put into a hot oiled skillet and brown slightly on both sides. Remove from pan & set aside. To same pan (leave all brownings in pan), add garlic, onion, peppers, mushrooms, parsley & basil. Sauté 5 min. Then add chicken, tamari and wine ~ cover and simmer 20 minutes.

~ Serve over rice or spinach noodles, with perhaps a green salad, bread and wine!

Chicken Moutarde

...unusual, and yet a very simple
and fast way to prepare chicken

1 chicken, cut up
1 lemon
½ cup Dijon mustard
½ cup honey
paprika

Wash chicken and pat dry. Place in
casserole dish — squeeze lemon
over chicken. Mix mustard and
honey together well and pour over
chicken. Sprinkle with paprika.
Bake at 350° for 40 minutes.
Place under broiler for 10 minutes
to brown, if you like... or else
just bake a total of 50 minutes.

Michael's Garlic-Tahini-Miso Chicken

4 boneless chicken breasts ~ cut into bite-size pieces
3 large cloves garlic, pressed
3 scallions, chopped
1 green pepper, chopped
½ lb. mushrooms, sliced
fresh or dried parsley
2 tbsp. butter
¼ cup miso (see pg. 234)
½ cup tahini (see pg. 237)
¼ cup water
a little freshly ground pepper

1 cup uncooked rice or 2 cups cooked rice

Cook rice as directed.
In a skillet, melt butter and sauté vegetables.
Add cup-up chicken and simmer 15 minutes.
Season. In a small pot mix tahini, miso and water ~ and slowly heat... Keep stirring to incorporate lumps of miso and tahini. When heated thoroughly but right before it begins to boil, remove from heat. Spoon chicken over rice and pour sauce on top. Serve.

Ricky's famous Chicken Cacciatore

3 whole boneless chicken breasts (or 6 halves)
1 cup flour
1 lemon
¼ cup olive oil
½ lb. mushrooms, slivered
1 onion, chopped
2 large cloves garlic, pressed
1 green or red pepper, chopped
½ cup white wine
1 medium can (crushed) Italian tomatoes
parsley – a bunch of fresh or 1 tbsp. dried
herb salt & pepper to taste
½ tsp. basil
½ tsp. oregano
3 cups cooked rice

Cut chicken breasts into bite-size pieces and squeeze lemon on top. Coat with flour. Heat oil in skillet and brown chicken lightly. Remove when finished. In same pan – add garlic, onion, green pepper and mushrooms. Sauté 10 minutes. Add chicken, salt & pepper, basil, oregano, parsley, tomatoes and wine. Cover and simmer 20 to 30 minutes.

Cook about 1½ cups brown rice (see pg. 233)

Serve on brown rice or pilaf.

Desserts

Carob or Chocolate Chip Cake

~ light ... a favorite ~!

- 3 cups flour
- ½ lb. butter or margarine
- 1 cup honey or maple syrup
- 3 tsp. baking powder
- 4 eggs, separated
- 1 cup milk
- 1 tsp. vanilla
- 1 pkg. (12 oz.) carob (sweetened) or chocolate chips ~ crushed

Preheat oven to 350°. Cream butter, honey and egg yolks together. Add vanilla. Sift dry ingredients and add to butter mixture a little at a time, alternating with milk. Keep beating. Crush chips in blender, food processor or by hand. Add ⅔ of crushed chips and mix well. Beat egg whites till stiff. Fold into batter. Spoon batter into buttered and floured tube pan. Sprinkle remaining chips on top.
Bake 1 hour at 350° or till tester comes out clean.

You'll love it !!
♡ ♡ ♡ ♡

Pumpkin Cake

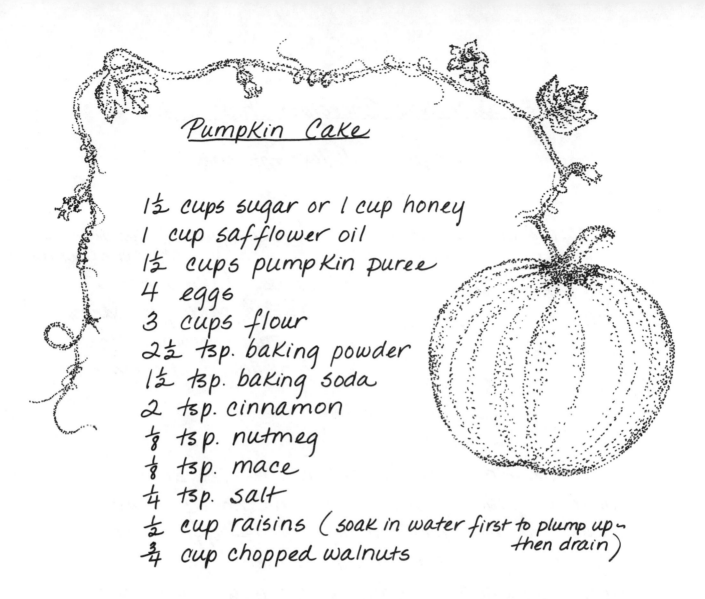

1½ cups sugar or 1 cup honey
1 cup safflower oil
1½ cups pumpkin puree
4 eggs
3 cups flour
2½ tsp. baking powder
1½ tsp. baking soda
2 tsp. cinnamon
⅛ tsp. nutmeg
⅛ tsp. mace
¼ tsp. salt
½ cup raisins (soak in water first to plump up — then drain)
¾ cup chopped walnuts

Preheat oven to 350°.
In a large bowl-mix sugar (or honey), oil and pumpkin, and beat until blended. Add 1 egg at a time, beating before adding each egg. Sift dry ingredients and add slowly, mixing well. Then stir in raisins and nuts.
Bake in a buttered tube pan 1 to 1½ hours at 350°. Do not open oven before 1 hour. Insert cake tester or dry knife to see when finished — should come out clean.

↪ This cake is good alone <u>or</u> with a dip of vanilla ice cream <u>or</u> topped with whipped cream!

Jude's Date · Nut · Chocolate Chip Cake

everyone will love this one !

1 cup chopped, pitted dates
1½ cups boiling water
1½ tsp. baking soda
1½ sticks butter, softened
⅔ cup honey
2 eggs

1¾ cups flour (W.W. or half unbleached white)
¾ tsp. baking soda
½ tsp. baking powder
1 cup chopped walnuts
8 to 10 oz. chocolate chips

Combine first three ingredients ∽ let stand ½ hour till cool. Cream butter and honey... add eggs and beat well till light and fluffy. Mix in cooled date mixture and blend well. Mix dry ingredients together (sift if you like, but it's not necessary) ∽ add dry ingredients to the batter and mix well until well blended, but do not overbeat. Stir in chopped nuts and chocolate chips. Pour into a buttered 9x13 cake pan.
Bake at 350° for 45 to 55 minutes or till cake tester comes out clean. Cool completely before slicing. Best baked the day before using, if possible. ♥

Dianne's
Gingerbread Cupcakes

Preheat oven to 375°.

Melt ½ cup butter or margarine and let cool.

Sift :
    2 cups sifted whole wheat flour
    ½ cup unbleached white flour
    1½ tsp. baking soda
    1 tsp. cinnamon
    1 tsp. ginger
    ½ tsp. salt
    1 tbsp. grated orange rind

Combine :
    2 eggs, beaten
    ½ cup light molasses
    ½ cup honey
    1 cup hot water

Add sifted dry and liquid ingredients alternately to the melted butter until blended. Add 1 cup chopped pecans.
Pour into cupcake shells — about ⅓ full.
Bake at 375° for 20 to 25 minutes.

Applesauce Spice Cake

quick & tasty ... no eggs

2 cups flour
2 cups applesauce (unsweetened)
1 stick butter (softened)
½ cup maple syrup
½ cup brown sugar
2 tsp. cinnamon
1 tsp. allspice
½ tsp. mace
1 tsp. vanilla
2 heaping teaspoons baking powder
½ tsp. salt
1 cup chopped walnuts
1 cup raisins (optional)

Preheat oven to 350°. Mix all dry ingredients together in a bowl. Cream softened butter with maple syrup, sugar and vanilla. Add applesauce. Mix well. Add to dry ingredients a little at a time. Beat well with a wooden spoon. Spoon into a buttered cake pan and bake 45 minutes to an hour at 350°. Check to see if done with a cake tester or knife.

Pineapple Cream Layer Cake

CAKE BATTER

3 cups flour (unbleached)
1 stick butter or margarine
1 cup maple syrup
2 large eggs
3 tbsp. baking powder
1 cup sour cream
1 to 2 tsp. vanilla

PINEAPPLE CREAM FILLING

1 13-oz. can crushed pineapple
1 cup heavy whipping cream
¼ cup maple syrup

Preheat oven to 350°. Grease and flour 2 layer cake pans.

In a bowl, cream butter, eggs, maple syrup and vanilla till light and fluffy... 5 minutes. Add flour and baking powder (I find it unnecessary to sift dry ingredients when using unbleached white flour ⌐ sift, if using whole wheat pastry flour), alternating with sour cream. Beat until fluffy. Spoon ½ of batter into each pan and bake at 350° for about 30 to 40 minutes, till golden, and a cake tester comes out clean when inserted. Let cool. Remove from pans.

To make filling ⌐ drain pineapple and mix with maple syrup. Beat cream till whipped... fold in pineapple mixture. Refrigerate until chilled. Spread ½ of filling on top of one layer. Add the top layer and cover with remaining filling.

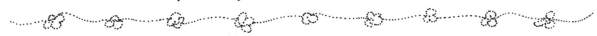

Nanny's Pound Cake

½ lb. butter

6 eggs

2 cups confectionary sugar

2 cups sifted flour

¾ cup milk, warmed

1 tsp. baking powder

1 tsp. vanilla

½ tsp. mace

Separate eggs and beat butter, yolks and sugar together. Beat whites until stiff and refrigerate till ready to use, to keep stiff. Heat milk.

Mix flour, milk, baking powder, vanilla & mace together ~ add butter, yolks and sugar... mix well. Fold in egg whites. Pour into buttered tube pan.

Bake at 350° for 1 hour. Use cake tester to make sure it's finished.

~ a sweet, old-fashioned family recipe ~

Strawberry Shortcake

~ there's nothing like it !

CAKE

3 cups flour
½ lb. butter
1 c. honey or maple syrup
3 tsp. baking powder
4 eggs, separated
1 cup milk
juice of 1 lemon
1 tsp. vanilla

TOPPING

1 cup whipping cream
1 tbsp. maple syrup
(add when whipping the cream)

fresh strawberries

Preheat oven to 350°. Butter and flour a tube pan. Cream butter, eggs, honey and egg yolks together. Add vanilla and lemon juice. Sift dry ingredients together. Add to butter mixture, a little at a time, alternating with milk. Beat egg whites till stiff. Fold into batter. Spoon into pan. Bake 1 hour or till tester comes out clean. Cool several hours. Remove from pan.

When ready to serve, wash and slice fresh strawberries. Whip cream. Place some berries and whipped cream on individual slices of cake.

NOTE
Cake will get soggy if you leave berries on top ~ so just use the berries when serving. Don't put on entire cake unless you know it will all be eaten immediately.

Linda's Cream Puffs

1 cup sifted flour
1 cup cold water
¼ tsp. salt

½ cup butter (salted)
4 large eggs
2 tsp. honey or
    maple syrup

Bring water, salt, butter and honey to a rapid boil. Add flour all at once. Remove from heat and stir until batter is stiff and forms into a ball. Put back on stove and heat for a minute or two. Remove and let cool several minutes. Beat each egg in, one-at-a-time, for one minute apiece and then after the last egg is in, continue beating a few more minutes. Let stand for one hour or so. Bake on lightly oiled cookie sheet (drop by tablespoonfuls or use pastry bag) at 450° for 20 min. Reduce heat to 350°. Bake 20 to 25 more minutes.

Filling:

2 cups milk
4 egg yolks
¼ cup honey or
    maple syrup

½ cup flour
½ tsp. salt
1 tsp. vanilla

1 8-oz. block of semi-sweet chocolate

Scald milk. Beat yolks & honey together w/ wire whisk. Add flour & salt. Slowly pour in hot milk, stirring constantly. Stir until thickened. Remove from heat. Pour into cold bowl. When cool, add vanilla. Slice off tops of puffs — fill and replace tops. Melt chocolate & drizzle over each puff. Refrigerate until ready to serve.

Grandma Jean's Apple Pie

... now, this is really {MOM'S APPLE PIE}
↳ right from our favorite Delhi Kitchen!
... a classic !!

8-10 apples
¼ cup flour
1 cup sugar
cinnamon
butter - (to be used later)

Peel and core apples, and cut into moderate chunks. Combine with remaining ingredients in bowl. Set aside.

To make crust:
2 cups flour, sifted
1¼ tsp. salt
⅔ cup shortening
-or almost a cup-
¼-½ cup ice-cold water

Cut shortening into flour — add water & mix till it all holds together. Wrap in wax paper and refrigerate 10 min. before rolling. Roll out and put in plate ... spoon apple mixture into crust. Dot with butter. Place remaining crust on top. Flute edges and prick top with fork.
Bake 45 minutes at 450°.

Chocolate and Carob Celebration Cake

or...
Compromised Decadence !

(↪ THE BEST OF TWO WORLDS ↩)

Cake
  1 cup unsweetened carob powder
  2 cups boiling water
  3 cups flour (unbleached white)
  3 tsp. baking powder
  ½ tsp. salt
  1 cup butter or margarine, softened
  1½ cups honey or maple syrup
  4 eggs
  2 tsp. vanilla

Frosting
  1 6-oz. pkg. semi-sweet chocolate chips
  ½ cup light cream
  1 cup butter or margarine, softened
  ½ cup honey or maple syrup

Filling
  1 cup heavy cream
  2 tbsp. honey or maple syrup
  1 tsp. vanilla

continued →

Preheat oven to 350° — butter and flour 3 9-inch layer cake pans.

Cake — Boil water. In a bowl combine carob powder and boiled water — beat until smooth. Set aside to cool. Sift dry ingredients. In a large bowl beat with a mixer or a strong hand... the butter, honey or maple syrup, eggs and vanilla till light and fluffy. Start adding dry ingredients, alternating with the carob mixture. Incorporate well but do not overbeat. Spoon evenly into the 3 cake pans and bake at 350° for 30 minutes. Check with a cake tester. Cool in pan.

Frosting — In a pot combine chocolate chips, cream, butter and honey. Melt, stirring often. Remove from heat... cool and re-frigerate 1 hour.

Filling — Whip the filling ingredients ... refrigerate.

When ready to assemble cake, remove cake from pans — place one layer on a plate ... spread with half of filling. Place 2nd layer on top — spread with rest of filling. Place 3rd layer on top and cover the entire sides and top of the cake with the chilled frosting. Refrigerate cake till ready to serve.

Penny's Evolved Jewish Applecake

easy and very delicious!

You can make this cake with just a wooden spoon — don't dirty the mixer.

4 to 5 sliced apples
1 tbsp. cinnamon
¼ cup honey

Slice apples into a bowl — add cinnamon and honey, and mix well. Set aside.

. . . .

Batter:

3½ cups flour
4 tsp. baking powder
1 tsp. salt

1 cup honey
1 cup oil (safflower is good)
1 cup orange juice
4 eggs
1 tsp. vanilla

. . . .

Put all batter ingredients in one bowl and beat with wooden spoon till well blended. Butter and flour a tube pan. Spoon half of batter into pan. Place ½ apple mixture on top, then spoon the rest of batter on top. Add remaining apple mixture. Push apples into batter slightly with spoon.
Bake at 350° for 1 hour 10 minutes or until tester comes out clean.

Great with tea or coffee... a big & beautiful cake!

Grandmom Mary's Orange Cake

Elegant!

Cake

3 cups flour
1½ cups orange juice (concentrated)
1 cup sugar
1 tsp. baking powder
1 tsp. baking soda
1 tsp. vanilla
1½ sticks butter or margarine
1 tsp. salt
2 eggs
1 cup raisins
½ cup walnuts, chopped

Topping

⅓ cup sugar
½ cup chopped walnuts
1 tsp. cinnamon

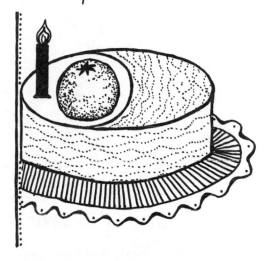

Preheat oven to 350°. Butter and flour a round cake pan or an 8x10 oblong pan. In a bowl-cream eggs, butter, sugar and vanilla together. Sift flour, salt and baking powder. Add to butter mixture, alternating with orange juice. Add walnuts and raisins. Blend well ~ do not overbeat. Spoon into pan. Bake at 350° for 1 hour or till tester comes out clean.

Topping —

Mix topping ingredients together... make holes in warm cake with a toothpick & sprinkle on topping.

Bobka

... a yeasted coffee cake

Takes me back to old Russia! An old
family recipe — _authentic_ and _delicious_!

1 stick butter, softened
½ cup sugar (or ¼ c. maple syrup or honey)
5 cups flour (½ unbleached & ½ W.W. is nice)
2 eggs
¾ cup lukewarm milk
½ cup lukewarm water
2 pkg. or 2 tbsp. dry yeast

Topping: 1 stick butter
1 cup sugar or ⅔ c. maple syrup or honey
2 tsp. cinnamon

In a small bowl, combine ½ c. lukewarm water with 2 tbsp. yeast
and a pinch of sugar. Set aside in warm place till it rises to top
of bowl (only need cup-size bowl). In a large bowl, beat with a
whisk or spoon, your stick of softened butter, 2 eggs & ½ cup
sugar. Mix a little, then add ¾ c. lukewarm milk & yeast mixture.
Add 4 c. flour and gradually knead in the remaining cup of
flour. Knead about 5 min. or so, till it feels smooth. Then put
back in bowl & cover with a towel, and refrigerate overnight. The
next morning, melt 1 stick butter — add 1 c. sugar and 2 tsp.
cinnamon. Mix well. Set aside. Remove dough from refrigerator
and divide into balls — each about the size of a walnut — or
just chunks (as Granny says!). Dip each chunk into melted
butter, sugar & cinnamon mixture, and sit side-by-side in a
round tube pan. Let rise 1 hr. in a warm place. Bake in an
_un_-preheated oven at 350° for 1 hour. Serve warm with butter...
with dinner or as a dessert.
 — It's wonderful with a little homemade jam & cream cheese!

serves 4

Creamy Rice Pudding

½ cup uncooked rice
2 cups milk
2 eggs, separated
¼ cup honey
¼ tsp. salt
1 tsp. vanilla
½ cup raisins (optional)
pinch of cinnamon

Place rice and milk in top of double
boiler. Cook – covered – 45 min. Beat
egg yolks, honey and salt together.
Stir some rice mixture into yolks.
Add yolks to hot mixture... cook 2 min.,
stirring constantly. Remove from heat.
Add vanilla. Whip egg whites till
fluffy. Fold into rice mixture. Add
cinnamon and raisins if desired.
Serve warm or chilled.

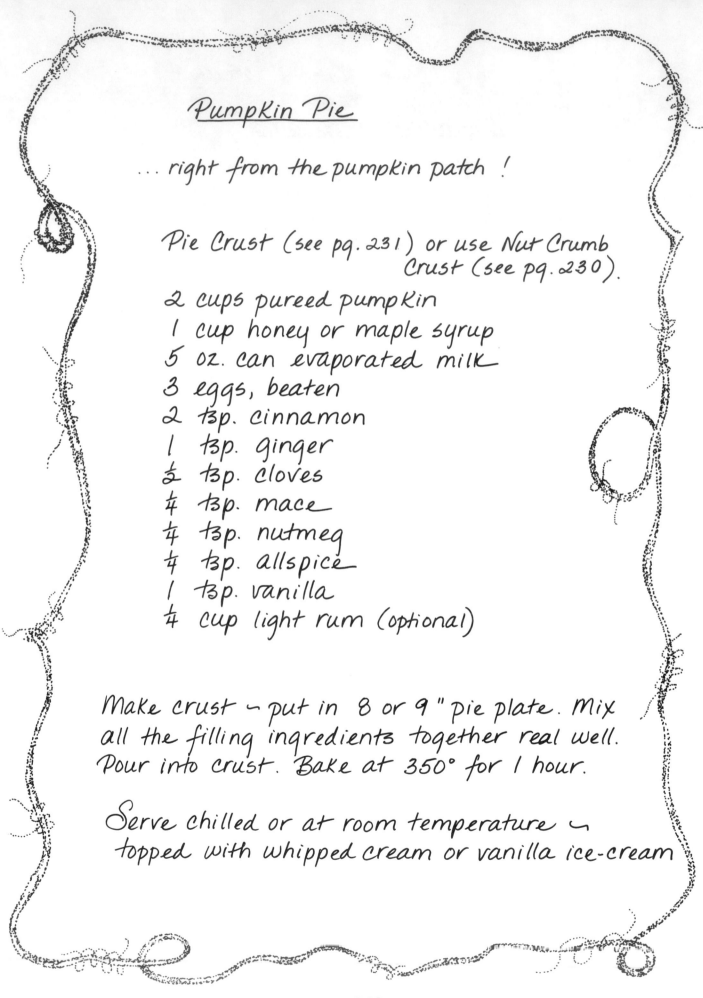

Pumpkin Pie

... right from the pumpkin patch!

Pie Crust (see pg. 231) or use Nut Crumb
Crust (see pg. 230).

2 cups pureed pumpkin
1 cup honey or maple syrup
5 oz. can evaporated milk
3 eggs, beaten
2 tsp. cinnamon
1 tsp. ginger
½ tsp. cloves
¼ tsp. mace
¼ tsp. nutmeg
¼ tsp. allspice
1 tsp. vanilla
¼ cup light rum (optional)

Make crust — put in 8 or 9" pie plate. Mix
all the filling ingredients together real well.
Pour into crust. Bake at 350° for 1 hour.

Serve chilled or at room temperature —
topped with whipped cream or vanilla ice-cream

Stewed Apples
excellent !

3 cups apples
¼ to ½ cup honey
2 tbsp. flour
1 cup water or apple juice
¼ cup milk
dash of salt
½ tsp. cinnamon
pinch of nutmeg

...serve as a dessert or as a savory side-dish...

Wash, pare and core apples. Cut into bite-size pieces. Place apples, water (or juice) & honey into a medium pot. Cook about 5 minutes. Stir. Add milk to flour and stir to a smooth paste. Add paste to apples ~ cook until slightly thickened, stirring constantly (about 2 minutes). Remove from heat ~ spoon into serving dish. Sprinkle with cinnamon and/or nutmeg.

Serve warm...
exquisite topped with vanilla ice cream!

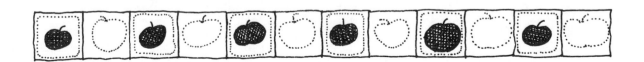

Apple Cobbler

∽ with vanilla sauce

Crust

1 stick butter
1 cup oats
2 cups flour
¼ cup honey
1 cup finely-
chopped walnuts

Apple Filling

8 lg. apples, peeled and
          chopped
½ cup raisins
½ cup honey
2 tsp. cinnamon
¼ tsp. mace
¼ tsp. orange rind
          (optional)

Vanilla Sauce

2 cups milk
½ cup honey
2 tsp. vanilla
2 egg yolks
2 tbsp. arrowroot
          flour

SEE PAGE 95
FOR DIRECTIONS

Crust:

In a medium sized pot, melt butter – add honey and stir. Add oats – mix. Add flour and walnuts and mix together with a fork till crumbly. Put half of crumbs in bottom of a large 9x13 baking dish.

Apples:

Peel, core and chop apples – add remaining filling ingredients... mix and spoon into crust in pan. Sprinkle remaining crumbs evenly on top. Put in oven and bake at 350° for 40 minutes.

Vanilla Sauce:

Follow directions on page 95 for cooking instructions.
Then – pour sauce over cobbler and bake 20 min. longer.
Serve warm or at room temperature... alone, or topped with vanilla ice-cream.

Grandmom Mary's Scottish Cookies

~makes 50 to 60 cookies~

NO EGGS... FOR YOU LOW CHOLESTEROL LOVERS!

2 cups flour
1 tsp. baking powder
1 tsp. salt
1 cup sugar
2 cups bran flakes
2 cups rolled oats
½ cup boiled water
½ tsp. baking soda
1¼ cup butter or margarine, softened
⅔ cup raisins
1 tsp. vanilla

PUT THESE COOKIES IN AN AIRTIGHT CONTAINER OR PLASTIC BAG AND KEEP FROZEN. THEY'RE BEST EATEN RIGHT FROM THE FREEZER!

Preheat oven to 400°. Boil ½ cup water and mix with ½ tsp. baking soda and let stand till cool. Meanwhile, mix all dry ingredients in a large bowl. Add softened butter and mix in with a slotted spoon. Add water, vanilla & raisins ~ mix till it comes together into a ball. Add a little more flour if needed so it doesn't stick to your hands. Knead for a minute or two. Divide in half... roll out on floured board and cut with a round cookie cutter. Place on an oiled cookie sheet. Bake at 400° for 10 minutes or till golden.

Great with a cup of tea ~ anytime of the day or night!

Old Fashioned Coffee Cake Goes Natural

this is a basic coffee cake usually made with sugar, which I converted to maple syrup ~ now it's even more delicious ... moister, yet light and fluffy.

Batter:
- 3 cups flour (unbleached white ~ or you can use ½ w.w. pastry flour)
- ½ lb. butter or margarine
- 1 cup maple syrup
- 2 eggs
- 3 tsp. baking powder
- 1 cup sour cream
- 1 tsp. vanilla

Topping:
- 1 cup chopped walnuts
- 1 tsp. cinnamon
- ¼ cup maple syrup

Preheat oven to 350°. Butter and flour a tube pan or a flat pan (whichever you prefer). In a bowl cream butter, eggs, maple syrup and vanilla till fluffy. Mix flour and baking powder and add gradually, alternating with sour cream. Beat well ~(I didn't even sift the dry ingredients and it came out light & fluffy)~ Spoon ½ batter into pan. Mix the topping ingredients together in a bowl and spoon ½ topping on batter in pan ~ then add remaining batter & rest of topping lastly.
Bake at 350° for 1 hour. Cake tester or dry knife should be inserted to test if done... it should come out clean.

...A WONDERFUL CAKE FOR A BRUNCH OR A TEA...

Divine Apple Cream Torte

pastry for 1 pie crust (see pg. 231)

5 or 6 large apples
8 oz. cream cheese
⅔ cup maple syrup
1 tsp. vanilla
1 egg
½ to 1 tsp. cinnamon
¼ tsp. mace or nutmeg (optional)
½ cup chopped walnuts
2 tbsp. maple syrup or sugar

Make crust as directed. Beat together cream cheese, egg, ⅓ cup maple syrup and vanilla. Pour into crust. Peel and slice apples – mix with ⅓ cup maple syrup and cinnamon. Spread on top of cream mixture. Mix chopped walnuts with 2 tbsp. syrup and sprinkle on top of apples. Bake at 350° for 50 minutes.

 Serve warm or at room temperature.

Lee's [Old-Fashioned] Shortbread Cookies

2½ cups flour
1 cup butter
½ cup sugar
1 tsp. vanilla
1 tbsp. milk

Put sugar and butter in a large bowl. Add vanilla. Beat with wooden spoon till fluffy and smooth. Then stir in flour and milk. Beat until smooth. Pat on a sugared pastry board or cloth. Shape into cookies or larger cakes (about 5 inches). Flute edges and prick with fork all over. Bake in 325° oven on ungreased cookie sheet until lightly golden brown. Do not let them get too dark. Cool on wire rack.

❤Sheryl's Pineapple-Blueberry Cheesecake

this is one of our favorite cheesecakes... it's very light and easy to make - great for a party, as it goes a long way.

Crust

¼ lb. butter or margarine
1 tbsp. sugar
2 cups flour
1 tsp. baking powder
2 tsp. vanilla
2 eggs

Fruit

1 8 oz. can crushed pineapple
1 cup blueberries, fresh or frozen
2 tbsp. corn starch
¼ honey

Filling

2 8-oz. pkg. cream cheese
1 tbsp. sugar or ¼ cup honey or maple syrup
2 tbsp. flour
1 tbsp. vanilla
juice of 1 lemon
4 eggs
4 cups milk
cinnamon

...juice and all!

Crust:
Cream together the butter, sugar, flour, baking powder, eggs and vanilla — then press with hands into a large baking pan.
(a 13"x9"x2" dish is good)

Fruit:
In a pot, mix pineapple, blueberries, cornstarch & honey together and cook 5 minutes or so, till it thickens. Pour into crust.

Filling:
Then, cream the cream cheese, sugar, flour, vanilla & lemon juice. Add eggs and milk — beat a minute or two till blended. Then pour into pan on top of fruit. Sprinkle with cinnamon and bake 1 hr. 10 min. at 325°.

Penny's Scrumptious Carrot Cake

⌣ with cream cheese icing... VERY EASY!

CAKE:

2½ cups flour (whole wheat pastry)
1 tsp. cinnamon
2 tsp. baking soda
4 tsp. baking powder
2 eggs
1 cup honey
1½ sticks butter
½ cup lemon juice
2 cups grated carrots
1 cup raisins
½ cup coconut
1 cup chopped walnuts

ICING:

8 oz. cream cheese
½ cup honey
1 tsp. vanilla
½ cup powdered milk
1 tbsp. lemon juice

Cream together butter, honey, eggs and lemon juice. Add dry ingredients. Beat well. Add carrots, raisins, coconut and walnuts. Blend thoroughly. Spoon into buttered flat Pyrex pan (13"x9"x2") or something similar. Bake at 350° for 30 to 45 minutes or till insert comes out clean.

Icing → soften 8 oz. cream cheese... mix with ½ cup honey, 1 tsp. vanilla, ½ cup powdered milk and 1 tbsp. lemon juice. Spread on cake when cooled.

Fanny's Fantastic Sweet Kugel ...

a noodle & cream cheese pudding ﹏

: A WONDERFUL DESSERT, SIDE DISH ... GREAT FOR A BRUNCH OR TEA .

Kugel

½ lb. fine egg noodles (if you can't get fine noodles, then crush up larger noodles)
½ lb. cream cheese
½ lb. creamed cottage cheese
1 cup sour cream
1 stick butter, softened
6 eggs, beaten
2 cups milk
¾ cup sugar or ½ cup honey
      or maple syrup

1 tsp. vanilla

Topping

1 stick butter
2 cups crushed graham
      crackers
8 tbsp. sugar or 4 tbsp.
      honey or maple syrup
1 tsp. cinnamon
      (optional)

Boil water for noodles. While water is coming to a boil, cream together cottage cheese, cream cheese, sour cream, butter, eggs, milk, sugar (or honey) and vanilla. Cook noodles (don't overcook). Drain and mix well with the cheese mixture. Pour into a buttered 9x13" baking dish...

To make topping — melt butter — add sugar or honey, graham cracker crumbs and cinnamon. Mix well till crumbly. Sprinkle on top of Kugel and bake at 325° for 1½ hours.

Serve warm or at room temperature... alone or topped with sour cream ﹏ ♡

Creamsicles

~ tastes like _the_ _real_ _thing_!
(... without all the artificial)
(colors and preservatives)

You will need something for making popsicles in... Tupperware makes a nice set. You can even use paper cups with a stick in the middle

- concentrated orange juice
- vanilla yogurt or vanilla ice cream

Fill popsicle holder with ⅓ orange juice. Place in freezer for 10 minutes or so, till it sets a little. Remove and put in some yogurt or ice cream (⅓), and pour remaining (⅓) orange juice in. Freeze well.

 .  .  .  .  .

~ The popsicles can be varied if you can find other fruit concentrates ~

NOTE: We really didn't go into the specifics of HOW MUCH orange juice and yogurt or ice cream to use, since it really depends on the size & number of popsicles you want to make.

Hawaiian Banana Ice Cream

this is dedicated to our friends
on Kauai, who make this
milkless wonder... ALOHA

or any
other
fruit!
FOR INSTANCE:
strawberries
oranges
blueberries
peaches
pineapples ~ consistency
etc.   will be more like
  etc.   sherbet
or... mix a few
together!
~ Let *your* imagination *go wild* ~

- Bananas (allow 1 per person)
- Honey or Maple Syrup
  (... just a dab ~ make sure to use
  ripe fruits. They're easier to
  prepare & are naturally sweet)
- Crushed Walnuts (optional)
- Dates, pitted (optional)
  or
- Raisins (they add little specks of sweetness)

Peel bananas and cut up in pieces. Put in freezer. Let
freeze a few hours, then place in a food processor,
blender or juicer, along with a few dates, and blend
thoroughly. Then put back in freezer till set. Scoop
into sundae dishes. Try pouring a little maple syrup
on top... add some crushed walnuts ~ for the
total natural dessert!

A real lusciously decadent possibility would be to
melt some chocolate over fruit... and don't forget
the whipped cream (Ha - Cha - Cha - Cha !!)

  ~ just discovered a wonderful carob topping...
    it's called JAKE'S. Ask for at health food stores

Glazed Blueberry Pie

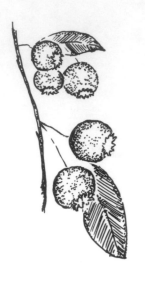

~ an incredible summer pie that requires only short oven time ... when it's too <u>hot</u> to cook, but not too hot to eat.

Crust for 1 pie (see pg. 231)

2 full pints fresh blueberries
⅔ cup boiling water
1 cup honey or maple syrup
3 tbsp. cornstarch or arrowroot (see pg. 233)
¼ tsp. cinnamon
a pinch of mace (optional)

Make crust as directed. Place in 8" or 9" pie plate. Prick holes in bottom with fork. Bake at 350° for 15 minutes or till golden. Cool.

While the crust is baking, wash your blueberries and mash about ⅓ of them. Place remaining berries in a good sized bowl. In a small pot, place <u>mashed</u> berries, boiling water, honey & cornstarch. Start to simmer ~ mixing constantly till thickens slightly (about the consistency of heavy cream). Remove from heat and let cool 5 min. Then, mix well with larger berries. Spoon into baked pie crust. Cool 20 min. ~ then refrigerate several hours. Serve chilled with freshly whipped cream or vanilla ice cream. ~ <u>Amazing</u>!

This pie can be made with <u>strawberries</u> or <u>peaches</u>, instead of blueberries ... or a combination of two fruits or more.

<u>FOR STRAWBERRY PIE ONLY</u> ... for severe decadence, we sometimes add 6 oz. of melted chocolate after the crust has baked and cooled. Simply melt your chocolate and pour into crust. Let cool till the chocolate hardens and then spoon in your strawberry filling. There's something about the strawberries & chocolate that is sublime ... which just doesn't happen with blueberries & peaches.

(Don't forget the whipped cream ~ it's essential!)

Strawberries & Sour Cream

… or Bananas
… or Blueberries
… or Peaches

⌐ while I was growing up, my mother made strawberries & sour cream for dessert quite often in the summer. It's so simple, yet a very special dessert!

Roughly:

1 pint of berries
1 pint of sour cream
¼ cup sugar or maple syrup

Wash your berries well. Remove stems and slice into halves … my mom used to sprinkle sugar on them; I like to use maple syrup … then refrigerate. (Cutting the berries early in the day and refrigerating makes them real juicy).

When ready to serve, mix with as much sour cream as you dare!

Superbowl Chocolate Cheesecake

Double the recipe for
      Nut Crumb Crust (see pg. 230)

1½ lbs. cream cheese
12 oz. semi-sweet real chocolate
1 cup sour cream
3 eggs
1 cup maple syrup or light honey
2 tsp. vanilla

Make nut crumb crust and spread onto bottom, by patting, of a large 9"x13" pan. Blend the above ingredients in a food processor or with a mixer till ingredients are well incorporated. Pour into crust and bake 1 hour. Cool and chill a few hours before serving.

Delightful Carob or Chocolate Chip Cookies

1 stick of butter or margarine, softened
$\frac{1}{2}$ cup honey
1 egg
1 tsp. vanilla
1 heaping cup flour
$\frac{1}{2}$ tsp. salt
$\frac{1}{2}$ tsp. baking soda
1 square semi-sweet chocolate or carob ground into a powder ~ or approximately $\frac{1}{2}$ cup chips
$\frac{1}{2}$ cup ground walnuts

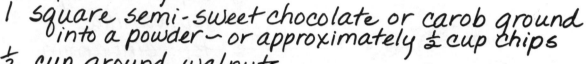

Preheat oven to 350° In a bowl beat butter, eggs and honey till fluffy. Add vanilla, flour, salt and baking soda (you can sift dry ingredients if you wish ~ I don't find it necessary in this recipe). Mix well. Put chocolate and nuts in a blender or food processor, and blend until powdery. Add to rest of ingredients and mix well. Spoon onto a buttered cookie sheet and bake 15 minutes or till golden.

Blueberry Sour Cream Crumb Pie

...Extraordinary!

Crumb Crust

1½ cups flour
1 stick butter
3 tbsp. maple syrup or
       honey

Pie

1 pint fresh blueberries
1 pint sour cream
2 eggs, beaten
⅔ cup maple syrup
1 tsp. vanilla
½ tsp. cinnamon
¼ tsp. mace (optional)

Crust:

Melt butter in a small pot. Add syrup or honey. Mix well. Add flour and mix with a fork till crumbly. Pat out ½ of crumbs in pie plate and save ½ for top of pie.

To make pie:

In a bowl, simply combine all the pie ingredients and mix well. Spoon into pie plate on top of crust. Sprinkle top with remaining crumbs and bake at 350° for 50 minutes.

Serve warm or chilled...
for sheer madness, top with a little whipped cream!

Hamantaschen — prune cookies

Myra and I made these traditional Jewish pastries one afternoon... We felt as though we were back in Russia! They were very delicious. You do it all in a big bowl with a wooden spoon and your hands... they didn't have electric cake mixers in those days! Perhaps that's why they're so-o-o good.

Cookie Dough

5½ cups flour
4 eggs, beaten
1 cup sugar
1 cup oil
juice & rind of 1 orange
2 tsp. baking powder
1 tsp. salt

Filling

1½ lb. prunes (soak for a couple hours – drain & remove pits..... or use already pitted prunes or see if you can find Lekvar Prune Butter at supermarket, to save time)
1 cup raisins
½ cup sugar
1 cup chopped walnuts
juice and rind of ½ a lemon
1½ tsp. cinnamon

In a large bowl, mix the dough ingredients well and chill while making the filling. To make filling: put all the filling ingredients in a food processor, or put in a wooden bowl and chop with a food chopper — and blend. Remove dough from refrigerator... roll out in small amounts. Take a glass and cut rounds of dough with top of glass — or, if you have a round cookie cutter, you can use that. Fill each round with about 1 tsp. filling (depending on size). With fingers pinch dough together in a triangle shape. Place on oiled cookie sheet and bake at 350° for 30 minutes.

Pumpkin Cheese Pie Supreme

try growing pie pumpkins ~ they store well
and will inspire you to bake pumpkin
pies throughout the year!

<u>Double</u> the recipe for pie crust
(see pg. 231)

2½ to 3 cups pureed pumpkin
1 lb. cream cheese
3 large eggs or 4 medium eggs
1 cup honey
2½ tsp. cinnamon
1 tsp. vanilla
1 tsp. ginger
½ tsp. cloves
¼ tsp. mace
¼ tsp. nutmeg
1 tsp. allspice
¼ tsp. orange rind (optional)

Blend all the above ingredients together in a
food processor or mixing bowl ~ and pour
into a pie crust (use a 9 x 13" Pyrex pan or
2 8-inch pie pans).
Bake at 350° for 1 hour.

Serve at room temperature ~ alone or
topped with whipped cream.

<u>Sharon's Popcorn Balls</u> or <u>Natural Cracker Jacks</u>

1 large pot of popped corn (about 5 or 6 qts.)
1 stick butter or margarine
½ cup honey
½ cup molasses
1 cup raisins
½ cup coconut (optional)
1 cup shelled peanuts and/or chopped
    almonds, pecans and walnuts

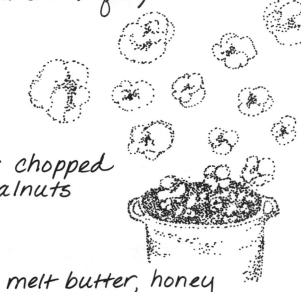

Pop your corn. In a small pot, melt butter, honey and molasses together, and bring to a boil. Continue cooking at a rolling boil (will look "frothy") until mixture thickens (can test by taking a metal spoon & dipping it in — then wave it in the air to cool down some. Then you'll be able to determine how thick it is). Give it a good 3 to 5 minutes. Meanwhile, add raisins, nuts and coconut to popped corn — then pour thickened mixture over that and mix well. It's best to get your hands right in there to make sure you get the peanuts and raisins off the bottom! If you want to make the balls, be sure to butter or oil your hands well and <u>squeeze</u> together real hard till it holds shape.

What a treat! And good for you, too!!
Serve at kids parties... for snacks... anytime!

my mother's Apple Strudel

<u>Dough</u> — same as Schnecken (see pg. 229)

<u>Filling</u> —
   4 or 5 large apples (my mom always used winesap apples)
   1 cup raisins
   1 cup chopped walnuts
   ½ cup shredded coconut (optional)
   1 cup strawberry jam

<u>For rolling out dough</u> —
   ½ cup flour
   ½ cup sugar
   1 tbsp. cinnamon

Make dough and refrigerate several hours or overnight. When ready to roll, first peel and slice apples — add raisins, walnuts, coconut and jam and mix well. Set aside. Then... mix ½ cup flour, ½ cup sugar and 1 tbsp. cinnamon together, and dust an area with same for rolling out dough. Take ¼ of the dough and roll out as thin as you can get it. Take ¼ of apple mixture and spread on rolled dough. Start rolling up like a jelly roll and place on an oiled cookie sheet. Repeat, using remainder of dough and mixture. Bake at 350° for 40 minutes.

Serve warm...Heavenly!

Schnecken

a very old family recipe ~ an incredible light pastry filled with raisins, nuts, etc.

... read on

Dough ~ prepare early in the day or day before

½ lb. butter, softened
1 cup sour cream
1 egg yolk
3 cups flour

Rolling-out "ingreds."

½ cup flour
2 tsp. cinnamon
½ cup sugar

Filling

1 cup chopped walnuts
1 cup raisins
½ cup grated coconut (optional)
1 cup strawberry jam
(I use jam made with honey)

Dough ~
Cream softened butter, egg yolk & sour cream. Gradually add flour till smooth. Knead 5 min. Divide into 4 balls. Roll each ball in flour, then place in plastic bag. Refrigerate several hours or overnight.

When ready to roll ~ combine all the filling ingredients together in a bowl. Mix well.

In another small bowl, combine rolling-out ingredients together & flour a wooden board surface with it. Roll out each ball on the floured & sugared surface into very thin circles (do one ball at a time). Cut into 8 triangular wedges △. Place a tablespoon of filling at wide end and roll up like a crescent. Place individual schneckens on an oiled cookie sheet. Bake at 350° for 25 to 30 min. or till golden. Serve at room temperature.

Nut Crumb Crust

½ cup crushed graham crackers
½ cup flour
1 cup finely chopped walnuts
              or almonds
6 tbsp. butter
2 tbsp. honey

Melt butter in a saucepan — add honey and mix well. Mix flour, crushed graham crackers and chopped nuts together... gradually add to butter and honey mixture, mixing with a fork till crumbly. Press into a 9" pie plate.

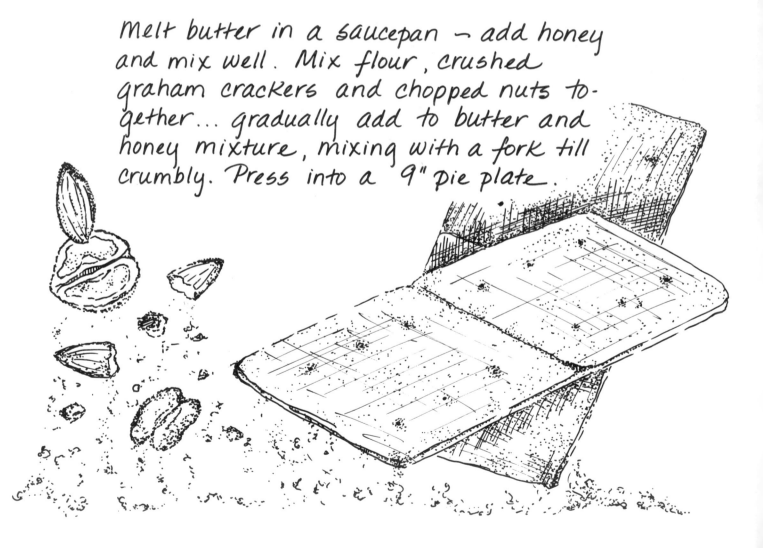

· for a one-crust pie ·

Our best <u>Pie Crust</u>

light & flaky ... never fails !

6 tbsp. butter (prefer lightly salted in this recipe)

1 heaping cup flour (use unbleached white, or ½
                     unbleached & ½ w/w pastry - see pg. 233)

2 or 3 tbsp. <u>ice-cold</u> water

Blend butter and flour well with
a pastry blender or fork ... till
it's the consistency of small
peas. Add water – a little at a
time – until it all sticks together.
Roll out.

... <u>FOOD</u> <u>PROCESSORS</u>
ARE GREAT FOR
MAKING CRUSTS...

Glossary

Apple Cider Vinegar...
is just that ~ vinegar made from apples. Delicious flavor and good for ya! Use in place of other vinegars in any recipe.

Arrowroot...
is a thickening agent similar to cornstarch. It is said that it has some medicinal properties. You can purchase it at most health food stores.

Brown Rice...
is the best rice to use as it is not highly processed and therefore has its vitamins and minerals intact. Sold at health food stores and most supermarkets.

Dr. Bronner's Liquid Bouillon...
this is similar to tamari, however it has several other natural ingredients which gives it a wonderful Oriental flavor. Nice in marinades and as a seasoning. Ask for it at your health food store.

Flours...
Unbleached White is wonderful for baking fine pastries and cakes. Whole Wheat is nice for breads. Whole Wheat Pastry is nice for cakes and pastries. Corn, rye and other heavier grains are used in bread recipes. Bleached white flour should be avoided, as most of its nutritional value has been destroyed by the processing methods.

"Herbamare" and other herb salts...
salt with several nice herbs added to it. Ask for them at health food stores and supermarkets.

Honey, Maple Syrup and Sugar...
Almost anything made with sugar can be made with honey or maple syrup. You will have to change the recipe slightly. Basically, if the cake calls for 1 cup sugar, I use between ½ to ⅔ cup honey or maple syrup. I prefer maple syrup for fine pastries, as it has a more delicate flavor than honey. They also both help in keeping a cake moist longer, and seems to be a natural preservative. Try experimenting with them both. To reduce the expense, I usually buy honey and maple syrup in large quantities.

Miso...
is a paste made of fermented soybeans, barley or rice ~ it is an excellent source of protein which can be added to soups, dressings & sauces.

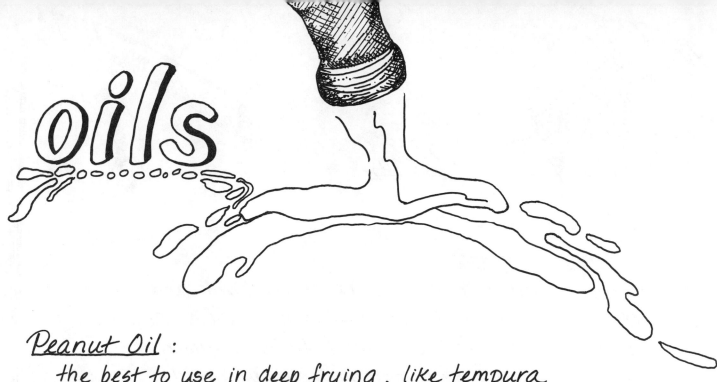

oils

Peanut Oil :
the best to use in deep frying , like tempura
and egg rolls ... it can stand the most heat
without burning. Hot oil must be the secret
to non-greasy foods.

Safflower Oil :
is a good all- around oil ⁓ good for salads,
baking and sautéing... has a very mild flavor.

Sesame Oil :
is nice to sauté in also ⁓ great for Chinese
and Japanese 'wok-ing.'

Olive Oil :
this is good in salads and for cooking Italian
foods ... Greek foods lend themselves well to
olive oil , too.

Corn Oil :
has a delicate flavor and can be used well in
pastries , cakes and breads.

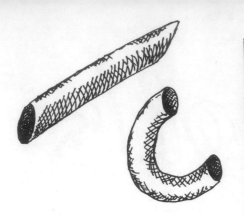

Pasta

Artichoke Pasta...

comes in all forms of pasta ~ it's light and very delicious, yet extremely nutritious, as it's made from Jerusalem Artichoke Flour. Sold at health food stores. Very special!

Sobo Noodles...

a Japanese pasta made with buckwheat flour. They are very tasty and good for you. Use in Oriental recipes. Sold at health food stores and Oriental markets.

Homemade Pasta...

if you've never tried it, you're missing something very special. Pasta is simple to make, and manual pasta machines are very inexpensive. If you have a food processor, it can be made in no time!

Tahini...
is a sesame butter — high in calcium. Wonderful in sauces & salad dressings. Sold at health food stores.

Tamari...
is basically the same as soya sauce but is naturally fermented and preserved, whereas commercially bought soy sauce has preservatives added to it. You can purchase at health food stores.

Tofu...
is made from soybeans. It is an excellent source of protein. It's bland in taste, however, it borrows flavors from whatever it is cooked with. It has no cholesterol and is very versatile. Try it .... we have grown to love it as we do fish and chicken.

Tofu Sauce ("White Tiger")... by Westbrae
a great bottled dark soya based sauce that has a wonderful Oriental flavor — which is good on chicken, tofu, rice and vegies ... ∞

T.V.P. (Texturized Vegetable Protein)...
is made from soybeans. They are granules that when soaked take on a chewy texture similar to ground meat. They are tasteless, but pick up the flavor of what they are cooked with. An excellent source of protein ... a wonderful addition to chili, soups & stews, lasagna, etc., where ground meat is usually used. Buy at health food stores.

INDEX